D0289425

AMERICAN ACADEMY OF PEDIATRICS

GUIDE TO YOUR CHILD'S SLEEP

CHILDCARE BOOKS FROM THE
AMERICAN ACADEMY OF PEDIATRICS

Guide to Your Child's Nutrition

Guide to Your Child's Symptoms

Your Baby's First Year

Caring for Your Baby and Young Child
Birth to Age 5

Caring for Your School-Age Child
Ages 5 to 12

Caring for Your Adolescent
Ages 12 to 21

AMERICAN ACADEMY OF PEDIATRICS

GUIDE TO YOUR CHILD'S SLEEP

Birth Through Adolescence

EDITOR-IN-CHIEF

George J. Cohen, M.D., F.A.A.P.
Professor of Pediatrics
George Washington University School of Medicine;
Senior Attending Pediatrician
Children's National Medical Center
Washington, D.C.

Villard
New York

Copyright 1999 by American Academy of Pediatrics

All rights reserved under International and Pan-American Copyright Conventions. Published in the United States by Villard Books, a division of Random House, Inc., New York, and simultaneously in Canada by Random House of Canada Limited, Toronto.

VILLARD BOOKS and colophon are registered trademarks of Random House, Inc.

ISBN 0-679-76981-1

Random House website address: www.atrandom.com

Printed in the United States of America on acid-free paper

987543

This book is dedicated to all the people who recognize that children are our greatest inspiration in the present and our greatest hope for the future.

From the Editor-in-Chief:
Special thanks to my four grown children, each of whose early sleep pattern was unique, and to my wife, Lenore, who patiently (but often sleeplessly) endured the variety.

Reviewers/Contributors

Editor-in-Chief
George J. Cohen, M.D.

AAP Board of Directors Reviewer
Eileen M. Ouellette, M.D., J.D.

American Academy of Pediatrics
Executive Director
Joe M. Sanders, Jr., M.D.

Associate Executive Director
Roger F. Suchyta, M.D.

Director, Department of Education
Robert Perelman, M.D.

Director, Division of
Public Education
Lisa R. Reisberg

Project Manager,
Division of Public Education
Brent L. Heathcott

Project Coordinator, Division of
Public Education
Kate Larson

Reviewers/Contributors
Javier Aceves, M.D.
F. Daniel Armstrong, Ph.D.
Lawrence Brown, M.D.
Heidi M. Feldman, M.D.

Peggy Gilbertson, R.N., M.P.H.
Joseph F. Hagan, M.D.
Barbara J. Howard, M.D.
John Kattwinkel, M.D.
Ana Navarro, M.D.
Anthony J. Richtsmeier, M.D.
Hyman C. Tolmas, M.D.
Mark L. Wolraich, M.D.

Acknowledgments
Editorial production by DSH
Editorial, Inc., a division of
G.S. Sharpe Communications, Inc.

Editorial Director
Genell J. Subak-Sharpe, M.S.

Managing Editor
Rosemary Perkins

Writers
Rosemary Perkins
Genell J. Subak-Sharpe, M.S.

Copy Editor
Karen Richardson

Designers
Tanya Krawciw
Debra Rabinowitz

Illustrator
Briar Lee Mitchell

Guide to Your Child's Sleep

PLEASE NOTE

The information contained in this book is intended to complement, not substitute for, the advice of your child's pediatrician. Before starting any treatment or program affecting your child's health and sleep, you should consult your own pediatrician, who can discuss your child's individual needs with you and counsel you about symptoms and treatment.

The information and advice in this book apply equally to children of both sexes. We have elected to alternate the use of "he" and "she" instead of using a single gender pronoun or the awkward "he/she" construction. When a problem is more common in one sex than the other, it is so indicated. Otherwise, you should assume that either gender can be equally affected, even though only one is referred to in the text.

FOREWORD

The *Guide to Your Child's Sleep* is the latest in a series of books for parents that has been developed by the American Academy of Pediatrics.

The American Academy of Pediatrics is an organization of 55,000 primary care pediatricians, pediatric medical subspecialists, and pediatric surgical specialists dedicated to the health, safety and well-being of infants, children, adolescents, and young adults. This book is part of the Academy's ongoing educational efforts to provide parents and caregivers with high-quality information on a broad spectrum of children's health issues.

What distinguishes this book from many other reference books in bookstores and on library shelves is that it has been written and extensively reviewed by pediatricians. Under the direction of our editor-in-chief, the material in this book was developed with the assistance of numerous reviewers and contributors from the American Academy of Pediatrics technical committees and sections. Because medical information about children's health is constantly changing, every effort has been made to ensure that this book contains the most up-to-date findings. Readers may want to visit the AAP website at www.aap.org to keep current on this and other subjects.

Another distinguishing characteristic of this book is its careful examination of conflicting sleep theories, which can enable parents to make the best decisions for their children and their families. The book explores several different approaches to a variety of sleep theories and offers proven strategies for helping newborns, toddlers, school-age children, and teenagers sleep soundly. The

Guide to Your Child's Sleep also takes a unique look at the role of parents in fostering a sound sleep environment for their children.

It is the Academy's hope that this book will become an invaluable resource and reference guide to parents. We are confident that parents and caregivers will find the book extremely valuable and we encourage its use in concert with the advice and counsel of readers' own pediatricians, who will provide individual guidance and assistance related to the health of children.

Joe M. Sanders, Jr., M.D.
Executive Director

AMERICAN ACADEMY OF PEDIATRICS

GUIDE TO YOUR CHILD'S SLEEP

Avoiding Bedtime Battles So the Whole Family Sleeps Well

Sooner or later, almost every parent must deal with a child's sleeptime problems. In early infancy, the first task is to help your baby learn to sleep longer at night and stay awake for increasingly longer periods during the daytime. A few months on, separation anxiety makes its first appearance. During this phase, which may come and go for at least a year and possibly much longer, parents have to persuade their child over and over again that they're around to protect him, that it's safe to go to sleep, that "Good night" doesn't mean "Good-bye forever!"

Other issues crop up throughout childhood. Each one is different, just as each child is unique. And yet the problems fall into predictable patterns, such as bedtime resistance, nighttime fears that keep a child sleepless, the midnight rambler who roams the house, the child who insists she can only sleep in her parents' bed. As each new problem arises, parents not only implore, "How can we get our child to sleep?" but also wonder, "When will *we* ever get a night's sleep?"

While sleep disturbances are common in childhood, they shouldn't be ignored. One study of 3-year-olds receiving treatment for sleep problems found that 84 percent of the children had had their problems since infancy. Another study showed that college students with sleep troubles had had similar difficulties since early childhood.

Unlike some minor behavioral issues, sleep problems usually don't just go away if you ignore them. Troubles with sleep can dog youngsters throughout the school years, causing difficulties with learning and behavior. The good news is that no matter what your family's specific problem may be, it's never too late to take steps to correct it.

Some sleep problems reflect normal stages in children's emotional and behavioral development. Provided a satisfactory routine was established early on, calm, loving reassurance may be enough to help get your child back into a habit of settling down to sleep.

Other problems stem from habits that may have been unintentionally fostered by parents or caregivers. In such cases, well-meaning efforts to help the child sleep have backfired, resulting in a child who resists going to bed, can't get to sleep on his own, has to be rocked to sleep, needs a bottle at night, wakes often during the night, or wakes up too early in the morning and looks for company.

In this book, a *Guide to Your Child's Sleep*, the members of the American Academy of Pediatrics share suggestions that have helped many of the families in their care. Pediatricians recognize that there is not always an easy answer to a sleep problem, and what works for one family may not necessarily be the answer for others.

Parents should feel free to adapt the Academy's recommendations according to the different temperaments and personalities of their children and themselves, as well as the many other factors that influence family dynamics. In this, as in other aspects of bringing up your child, trust your instincts and listen to your child. You know your own child better than anyone. Finding a solution that suits your family's style will make everybody happy and ensure restful nights.

In preparing a *Guide to Your Child's Sleep*, Academy members received invaluable help from parents, caregivers, and children who responded to our sleep survey website. The same themes recurred again and again:

"How do I get my baby to sleep in her own bed?"

"When will my toddler stop waking up several times a night?"

"Why does my child wake up too early every morning?"

"What's the best way to deal with persistent bed-wetting?"

"Where do nighttime fears come from?"

"My child's schedule is all mixed up; how do I get him to sleep at night and stay awake for school?"

Other frequently asked questions probed the pros and cons of the family bed for young families, sleep changes in the teenage years, and how much sleep is needed for rest and repair at the various stages of childhood.

We have included many of these questions, together with our contributors' recommendations, as framed boxes alongside the text. Not every question could be reprinted, due to the large numbers received, but we selected at least one from each category to ensure that problems were addressed from as broad a viewpoint as possible.

In this book we recommend strategies for establishing lifelong habits of restful sleep. These suggestions reflect our experience not only as pediatricians, but also as parents who have survived many sleepless nights and groggy days. Our suggestions take account of parents' need for sleep, which is too often overlooked. Sleep-deprived parents and crotchety babies don't make a happy combination.

This book deals extensively with the early childhood years, because that's when problems are most common and when parents feel most in need of sleep. However, sleep troubles in the school years and in adolescence are also covered. Here and there, we have repeated information as it applies to the different ages and stages of childhood. This repetition together with a detailed index and extensive cross-referencing will, we hope, make it easier for parents to refer to the book as new issues arise.

The information in this guide has been reviewed by many experts and represents the consensus of the 55,000 pediatricians who are members of the American Academy of Pediatrics. Members include pediatricians, pediatric medical subspecialists, and pediatric surgical specialists.

Not only are they physicians concerned with the health and well-being of children and young people, but the overwhelming majority are also parents who have to deal with the same childhood issues—in colicky infants, wakeful toddlers, resistant school-age youngsters, and sleepy adolescents—that every parent and caregiver must handle. The advice in this guide comes, therefore, from their experiences both as trained medical specialists and as sometimes exhausted, occasionally perplexed, and always loving and fulfilled parents.

Sleep, my child, and peace attend thee
All through the night.

George J. Cohen, M.D., F.A.A.P.
Editor-in-Chief

CHAPTER 1

Understanding Sleep

Although medical scientists still do not fully understand all of the functions of sleep, its benefits are obvious. After a good night's sleep, we awaken feeling rested, refreshed, and alert. The events we experience during waking hours are integrated into our memory as we sleep. Minor aches and pains often disappear during sleep, which gives the body time to repair some of the minor wear-and-tear damage to muscles and other structures.

Sleep becomes something of an obsession with many new parents. Not only do they worry about whether their baby is getting enough (or too much) sleep, but they also have concerns about their own lack of sleep.

The effects of insufficient or disturbed sleep are also quite obvious. From time to time, everyone stays up too late or suffers a sleepless night and then feels groggy and out of sorts the next day. Children who chronically fail to get enough sleep do not learn as well as better-rested youngsters. They also have a higher rate of behavior problems. In many cases, overtired children resort to hyperactivity and difficult behavior as a way of fighting off daytime drowsiness.

For parents of newborns or older children with poor sleep habits, the effects of not getting enough sleep can become a constant source of stress. Indeed, new parents often say that chronic lack of sleep is one of the most trying aspects of adjusting to parenthood. In the following chapters, you'll find practical advice

Sleep is one of the many body functions that are regulated by an inborn biological clock. Medical scientists believe that this clock is centered in two tiny clusters of cells, called the suprachiasmatic nuclei (SCN), located above the crossing of the optic nerves in the hypothalamus, deep in the central part of the brain. This biological clock is set according to certain environmental cues, especially the periods of daylight and darkness.

The typical human sleep/wake cycle is but one of a number of rhythmic cycles that take about 24 hours to complete; others include a variety of metabolic

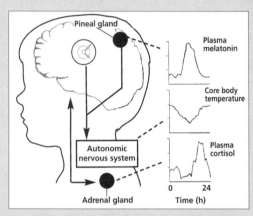

functions, slight shifts in blood pressure and body temperature, and the secretion of certain hormones. Technically, these 24-hour cycles are referred to as circadian (from the Latin meaning "about the day") rhythms. Circadian rhythms are part of our genetic makeup, and they help us stay in sync with the world around us. And the body's circadian clock must be set, like a watch, to local time. Travelers who rapidly cross several time zones usually experience jet lag, in which their biological clocks are at odds with the local time. The body automatically resets its clock, but, depending upon how many time zones have been crossed, it may take several days to do so. Although circadian rhythms are inborn, they take time to develop. This is why young babies have such erratic sleep/wake cycles. At about 6 weeks of age, circadian rhythms begin to develop, and by 4 to 6 months, most babies are on a regular sleep/wake cycle. It still may not match that of their parents and older siblings, but it pretty much follows a 24-hour pattern.

on how to deal with common sleep problems and help you and your entire family get a good night's rest. First, however, let's consider some of the basics about sleep.

To Sleep, Perchance to Dream

Virtually every living creature needs to sleep—at least some of the time. And each creature seems to have its own unique sleep pattern. Many of these patterns have evolved over the eons as a response to environmental factors. For example, many creatures share our human preference for sleeping mostly at night, when it is dark, quiet, and relatively safe. But night hunters, such as many of the wild cats, sleep mostly during the day and are awake and active at night, when their prey is easier to catch. Still others doze off periodically both day and night.

The amount of time spent sleeping also varies greatly. Domestic cats, for example, can sleep 20 or more hours a day, with many short naps interspersed between longer snoozes. Dolphins, mammals that, like whales, once lived on land but returned to the water, have developed a unique sleep pattern. In contrast to land mammals, these aquatic mammals need to control their breathing voluntarily when surfacing for air. Dolphins sleep with just one side of the brain at a time, periodically surfacing for air and alternating sleep sides until they have fulfilled the day's sleep needs. Then there are the birds, whose sleep includes brief flashes of the kind of nerve activity associated with rapid eye

Mothers Regulate Circadian Rhythms in Unborn Babies

Unborn babies are not exposed to light and have no means of telling day from night. Nevertheless, signals from the mother induce the baby to follow its mother's circadian rhythms. The mother's rising and falling levels of melatonin, the timekeeping hormone, pass across the placenta and help to regulate the biological clock in the baby's brain. This helps the baby adjust to regular daily rhythms after the birth.

movement (REM) sleep in higher animals (see next section). If birds had complete, prolonged REM sleep with its accompanying muscle paralysis, they would topple off their perches. Reptiles, fish, insects, and worms have periods of apparent rest during which sensory stimuli have to be stronger to make them react. However, although these creatures have sleeplike periods, their nervous systems and metabolisms do not change to sleep patterns as defined in higher animals. Humans and most other land animals have different stages of sleep, which range from light and partially awake to a state of unconsciousness so deep that it is often described as "dead to the world."

THE STAGES OF SLEEP AND SLEEP CYCLES

There are two basic types of sleep: REM (rapid eye-movement), the "active" sleep when dreams take place; and non-REM, or "quiet" sleep, which is divided into four stages. Each stage is marked by changes in brain waves, muscle activity, eye movements, heart function, and breathing, all of which can be measured by special instruments. Alternating cycles of non-REM and REM sleep make up the sleep stages that occur throughout the night.

Following is a summary of the typical sleep patterns of adults and children over the age of 3 or 4 years.

STAGE I is the brief period (up to 5 minutes) of transition from drowsiness to sleep. Brain activity slows and the eyelids close although the eyes continue to move together slowly beneath the closed lids. A person is easily awakened, often with a start, from this stage. Sometimes he may be aware that he is nodding off; at other times, he may think that he is only daydreaming rather than falling asleep.

Electroencephalograph recording of brain wave pattern, stage I: drowsiness

STAGE II is referred to as light sleep and lasts from 10 to 45 minutes. The brain waves begin to change with the appearance of vertex waves and K-complexes—large, slow waves interspersed with bursts of rapid waves called sleep spindles. K-complexes occur in response to environmental stimuli, and can be followed by arousal.

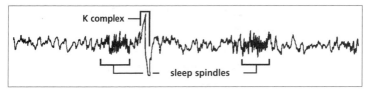

Electroencephalograph recording of brain wave pattern, stage II: light sleep

STAGE III marks the transition to a deeper state of sleep. There is a further slowing of the brain waves, and breathing and heartbeat become slow and regular. The muscles relax, and the person lies very still, although there may be some involuntary twitching of the legs. Some people begin to sweat; snoring may also occur.

STAGE IV flows smoothly from stage III, and marks the deepest state of sleep. The person is not easily awakened from stage III or IV sleep, and if roused, usually takes a minute or so to become fully awake. Taken together, stages III and IV may last up to 60 minutes. There is then a gradual return to a lighter, stage II sleep.

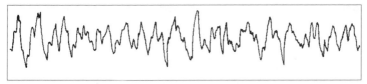

Electroencephalograph recording of brain wave pattern, stage IV: deep sleep

REM SLEEP AND MEMORY

The results of studies in animals and humans indicate that sleep deprivation interferes with the way in which recent experiences are integrated into long-term memory. As memories form, the connections between brain cells change. It is possible that the bursts of nerve activity that occur during REM sleep promote the changes in the brain cell connections and thus foster the formation of memories.

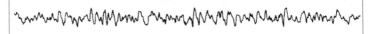

Electroencephalograph recording of brain wave pattern, REM sleep: dreaming (similar to Stage I)

REM SLEEP occurs after one or two complete cycles of stages I through IV sleep. Often referred to as "active sleep," this is the stage during which most dreams occur. The eyes move rapidly under the closed eyelids, breathing and the heartbeat become less regular, and the muscles are more relaxed, although twitching may increase. The first periods of REM sleep of the night usually last for only a few minutes; as the night goes on, however, REM sleep lengthens. This is why many people awaken in the morning while dreaming, and may feel as though the entire night has been spent dreaming.

Electroencephalograph recording of brain wave pattern, waking: eyes closed

SLEEP CYCLES Normal adult sleep is marked by recurring cycles of stages III and IV sleep (also referred to as slow-wave sleep), or even the lighter stages I and II, followed by varying periods of REM sleep. (These short, recurring cycles are referred to as ultradian rhythms.) Each cycle lasts an average of 90 minutes, although this varies from one person to another, and even from one night to another. For example, a person who has gone for several nights without getting enough sleep is likely to spend more time in REM and stages III and IV sleep than someone who has been sleeping well.

INFLUENCE OF AGE

As people grow older, sleep patterns and circadian rhythms change. For example, many adolescents experience difficulty falling asleep and prefer to awaken late. This is a chronobiologic disturbance called "delayed sleep-phase syndrome." It is not merely a result of teenage rebellion, but a reflection of altered release of melatonin, the timekeeping hormone (also see p. 71), during puberty and young adulthood. Many elderly people experience the opposite: early morning insomnia in which they wake up at 3 or 4 A.M. and can't go back to sleep. Even if they resist napping during the day, they often experience daytime sleepiness and want to go to bed early. Other biological rhythms, such as shifts in body temperature and hormone secretion, are also disrupted. Scientists do not fully understand why this happens, but many theorize that it is due to a loss of nerve cells from the suprachiasmatic nuclei (SCN; see *Biological Clocks*, p. 6).

Pre-Birth Workout

Even though a fetus spends most of its time asleep, an unborn baby is more active while asleep than adults are, which explains why mothers-to-be may feel kicking at all hours of the day and night.

How a Baby's Sleep Is Different

The sleep of newborn babies is quite different from that of adults and older children. Before circadian rhythms develop (see *Biological Clocks*, p. 6), newborns typically sleep for 2 or 3 hours at a time, wake up, eat, and soon fall asleep again. They usually sleep a total of 16 to 18 hours a day, with periods of sleep about equally divided between day and night.

Although newborns' sleep cycles appear to be random and erratic, the sleep itself follows a pattern, which begins to develop even before birth. Studies indicate that early in the third trimester of gestation, or at about the seventh month of fetal development, babies begin to experience active, or REM, sleep. A month or so later, quiet, or non-REM, sleep develops. After birth, you can easily tell the difference between the two types of sleep. During

REM Sleep: A Window on Brain Development

Sleep researchers have found intriguing links between REM sleep and brain development. Prolonged periods of REM sleep occur only in mammals, the animals (including humans) at the top of the evolutionary tree. Mammals have the largest and most highly developed brains. In particular, mammals have the highest proportion of neocortex, the part of the brain involved in reasoning. The neocortex is present, but very small, in fish and reptiles. It's a bit larger in birds, which evolved later and which also have brief bursts of brain activity consistent with REM sleep.

During REM sleep, a structure at the base of the brain sends out nerve impulses that travel throughout the brain and stimulate development of the structures involved in higher functions. One such structure is the cortex, where we do most of our thinking. The reason babies spend such long periods in REM sleep may be that it keeps the brain active, encourages the development of binocular vision, and ensures more stimulation (leading to growth) than babies can get from their senses while awake.

REM sleep, an infant may twitch or flail her arms or legs, and you can see her eyes move under her thin eyelids. Breathing may be somewhat irregular, and she may smile or make sucking motions with her mouth. As in adults, infants' non-REM sleep is deeper than their REM sleep; breathing is more regular and the baby will not move as much, although she may occasionally twitch or make a sudden movement.

Unlike adults and older children, newborn babies fall directly into REM sleep, a pattern that continues until they are about 3 months old. At first, sleep is about evenly divided between REM and non-REM, but this quickly falls to a ratio of 25 percent REM:75 percent non-REM in an older child or adult. Researchers believe that REM sleep plays an important role in

Sleep scientists thus theorize, on the basis of many years' research, that infants spend more time in REM sleep (about twice as long as young adults do) because it is critical for the development of the brain. We know that brain development is stimulated by nerve impulses triggered by our senses—sight, hearing, smell, taste, and touch. These nerve impulses are already at work while the fetus is growing in the mother's womb and continue after the baby is born. For example, even in the darkness of the womb, the eyes of the fetus create internal nerve signals, just as if they were activated by light. The nerve signals pass from the retina to the areas of the brain involved in vision and set up the stimulation that will be needed to form images when the time comes. This is the amazing system that allows a baby's eyes and brain to function immediately after birth. Nerves that fail to receive adequate stimulation during critical periods never develop properly. In the rare babies born with certain severe visual defects, for instance, the part of the brain responsible for vision will not develop unless the visual defect can be corrected soon after birth.

brain development, but its exact function is unknown. (See box, *REM Sleep: A Window on Brain Development*.) As the baby grows and the brain becomes more developed, progressively less time is spent in active REM sleep.

At about 2 months of age, your baby's sleep patterns begin to shift. Sleep becomes more consolidated, and a preference for nighttime sleep begins to develop. It's important to remember, however, that no two babies are exactly alike, and this is certainly true when it comes to sleeping. At 2 months, some babies are sleeping for stretches of 5 or 6 hours or more at night, while others are still waking up and wanting to be fed every 2 or 3 hours. Typically, however, by 2 or 3 months of age, most infants are sleeping for longer periods during the night, and staying awake

Sweating in a Sleeping Baby

 When I go to kiss my child after she's asleep, I find her damp with sweat. Is this normal?

Some people sweat during stages III and IV, the deepest stages of non-REM sleep (see p. 9). During these stages, a sleeper has regular, steady breathing and heart rate. Our bodies experience the most restorative effects of sleep at these times. You may find that your baby sweats until her clothes are damp. Usually, this is quite normal and no action is required. However, check to make sure that your baby is not overdressed, and that she is not overheated because, for instance, the room is too warm. Also check that your baby is not in any distress and that she does not seem to have a high fever. If all is well, simply wipe off your baby's brow and head to prevent her from becoming chilled and let her continue sleeping.

for much of the day, establishing a pattern that carries through until old age, when circadian rhythms may again shift.

CHAPTER 2

How Much Sleep
Does My Child Need?

"My first child is as regular as clockwork. He always gets drowsy as soon as his head hits the pillow, even if he's had a long afternoon nap. The next morning, he wakes up bright and early on his own, ready to start the day.

"My younger son is a wild man; for every minute he naps during the day, you can take a quarter-hour off his nighttime sleep. At bedtime, he always brings up an endless list of important things to tell us, gets up several times to use the bathroom, often needs to have monsters banished from the closet, and fights sleep every inch of the way. Almost every morning he has to be shaken awake and stays grouchy until after he's had something to eat."

If there's a lesson to be learned here, it's that every child is different. All children have the same basic needs for love, food, and sleep, although the amounts of food and rest vary, and they express their needs in different ways. Nevertheless,

Most parents are prepared for the fact that they will be getting up several times a night once they welcome a new baby into their home. What's surprising for many, when they look back, is how short a time the broken nights lasted. For the family's sake, it's important to help young children learn to sleep well, because overtired parents and fussy babies are not a happy combination. Good sleep habits let your children enjoy their days to the full.

characteristic patterns occur at the various stages of childhood. (Read about children's nutritional needs and eating patterns in the *American Academy of Pediatrics Guide to Your Child's Nutrition*, William H. Dietz, M.D., Ph.D. and Loraine Stern, M.D., editors, Villard, New York, 1999.)

Children's need for sleep generally falls within a range of hours that is linked to age. In general, age and developmental level are closely related. Exceptions have to be made for premature babies. Their developmental age is calculated from the day the baby "should" have been born, and not from the actual birthday (also see Chapter 9, "Twins and More"). From one age to the next, premature babies are much more variable in their sleep/wake development than term infants, although all healthy babies vary, within a wide normal range, in their sleep and activity patterns.

CYCLES START BEFORE BIRTH

Even unborn babies have sleep/wake cycles. Expectant mothers are aware that their babies' activity does not occur at random. Toward the end of gestation, an unborn baby may "wake up" and become particularly active at about the same early hour every morning (often well before his mother feels like getting up) with alternating periods of rest and exercise throughout the day. There may be another intense workout at a time when his mother is also very active. Unfortunately, your baby may not adhere to the same predictable sleep/wake schedule after he is born.

THE FIRST SIX MONTHS

Most newborn babies are sleeping or drowsy for 16 to 20 hours a day. Some wake at fairly regular 2-hour intervals, whereas others may occasionally sleep as long as 4 or 6 hours at a stretch. It's difficult to place newborns on a strict schedule, because their internal clocks are not yet functioning. At about 6 weeks, the daily cycles we call circadian rhythms (p. 6) start to become estab-

Healthy, growing babies do not need to be awakened to breastfeed or take a bottle. Check with your pediatrician about nighttime awakening if your baby is not doing the following:

• Feeding well five to eight times a day.

• Urinating normally with at least four wet diapers a day.

• Having normal bowel movements.

• Growing and gaining weight steadily.

lished. By about 16 weeks, many babies are very regular, what we call "entrained," or adapted to a light/dark schedule. They sleep more at night and remain alert for increasingly longer periods in the daytime. This rhythm comes about, in part, thanks to behavioral clues from the parents and caregivers, who encourage the baby to play more during the daytime waking periods. By contrast, nighttime wakings should be kept calm, quiet, and no longer than necessary to change, feed, and burp the baby and return him—comfortable, sleepy, but still awake—to his crib or bassinet. (For detailed information about the right way to position your baby for sleep, see pp. 44–46.) Even as babies become more alert and playful, many continue to take two or more daytime naps for at least the first 6 months. The morning nap gradually drops out but, for most children, the afternoon nap continues

GOOD NIGHT, MOON...

Even as early as 6 to 8 weeks you can establish a predictable bedtime routine: wash and change into sleepwear, a few minutes "reading" a picture book, a gentle song, saying good night to toys or pictures in the room. Activities performed in the same order each night make up a soothing ritual that helps put your baby in the mood for sleep.

Night Waking in a Good Sleeper

? *My 6-month-old baby used to sleep all night but suddenly, without any reason, is waking in the middle of the night. He is not teething, hasn't been sick, and is growing and developing well. What could be the cause?*

Waking phases come and go, often without any explanation, in the first few years. As long as your baby is healthy, well fed, and comfortable (bedroom not too warm or cold, diaper not soaked and clammy), this may be just a stage in his development. It is also likely that your baby is experiencing the onset of separation anxiety, a normal developmental stage in which the child fears the loss of his primary caregiver and becomes wary of unfamiliar faces. During this period, infants and toddlers often wake once or many times in the night and may even call for one parent in preference to the other.

When your baby cries, give him a few minutes to settle down on his own. If the crying continues, keep the lights dim as you check to make sure everything is all right, pat your baby and reassure him but avoid picking him up, and leave his room again as soon as he is calm but still awake. During the daytime, play lots of variations on "peek a boo" to help your baby develop confidence and anticipate your return.

through toddlerhood and into the preschool years. If, after the first few weeks, your baby is constantly drowsy, sleeps most of the time, and never seems fully awake, consult your pediatrician.

SIX TO TWELVE MONTHS

By the time your baby is 6 months old, you may expect her to take two naps totaling 3 to 4 hours during the day and to sleep

AN INFANT WHO WON'T LIE DOWN

 My 8-month-old gets so tired that he falls asleep sitting up in his crib. How can I get him to lie down before he falls asleep?

You don't have to force your baby to lie down. By now he has good enough motor control that after tumbling to the mattress, he can find a comfortable position for himself and sleep soundly the rest of the night.

for about 11 hours at night. For some lucky parents, the 11 hours will occasionally take place in a single stretch. At this age, babies are wide awake and active during play periods and usually sleep well after interludes of intense activity. Between 6 and 10 months babies typically try to pull themselves upright on furniture and in their cribs. They tire themselves out with the intense physical effort and concentration needed to master these and other complex movements, such as rolling over, reaching, and attempting to become mobile while crawling.

However, more broken nights are probably in store with the appearance of separation anxiety during the second half of the first year. Somewhere between 6 and 12 months, your infant, who used to be outgoing and friendly even with people he didn't

GAMES TO REINFORCE A SENSE OF IDENTITY

By about 8 months, a baby begins to look in the mirror in a different way, as he wakes up to the realization that the baby in the mirror is himself. You can strengthen your baby's growing sense of identity by playing games with him. When you're looking in the mirror together, touch different parts of your faces: "Johnny's nose...Mommy's nose..." or play peek a boo with the reflection, moving into and away from the mirror.

SECURITY BLANKETS = STRESS BUSTERS

The period between 8 and 15 months is usually the time when children become attached to transitional objects—cuddly blankets, toys, or sometimes unusual choices that help them make the emotional passage from dependence to independence. The presence of a comforting, familiar transitional object helps your child feel at home in a strange place, reassures him when he's away from you, calms him when he's upset, and helps him relax into sleep. It's a good idea to help your child blend a transitional object into his bedtime ritual by keeping a small, cuddly blanket or very small, soft toy in the crib.

For many children, a pacifier is the favored transitional object. Some pediatricians advise parents to wean children from pacifier use before this period. Language begins to develop about this time, and a child with a pacifier constantly in his mouth may not babble and speak as much as other children.

If the transitional object also becomes an indispensable daytime companion, as many do, you may want to keep a duplicate so you can wash and dry one while the other is on duty. A transitional object is a stress buster that the child will gradually give up on his own as he finds more mature ways to deal with life's challenges.

know, may start to become tense and fearful when strangers come too close. He may even get upset at the sight of family members or regular baby-sitters, especially if they approach abruptly. At the same time, he'll cling when you have to leave him or pass him to someone else to hold. If he finds himself in unfamiliar surroundings, he may appear uneasy and look to you for reassurance. This is separation anxiety, a normal phase and an important step forward in your child's emotional development. It indicates that your baby is becoming aware of himself as an individual separate from you. He is also beginning to understand that you, too, are a separate person. Separation anxiety generally peaks between 10

CHANGING A TRANSITIONAL OBJECT

? My 16-month-old uses my hair as a comfort object and continually runs his hands through it to fall asleep when he wakes in the middle of the night. How can I get him to learn to comfort himself on his own?

Because your toddler is used to the texture and odor of your hair, he may more easily accept a transitional object that simulates one or both of those features. Try giving him a small furry teddy bear or another cuddly toy, and dress it in one of your old T-shirts or another worn-out garment to convey your comforting scent. When he wakes in the night, check that he is comfortable, then go back to your own bed. The more you pick him up and linger, the more you encourage him to play with your hair.

and 18 months and gradually fades away during the latter half of the second year. Babies in this period often call out or cry for their parents in the middle of the night. Sometimes, they are able to pull themselves up to stand in their cribs, but can't get back down. They need help to reposition themselves for sleep (also see p. 171). Keep interactions with your child loving, supportive, brief, and matter-of-fact. Check with your pediatrician for additional strategies to reduce the duration of this phase.

During the separation-anxiety phase, your baby may also become fearful around objects and situations he used to take for granted. For example, his nighttime awakenings may be complicated by fear of the dark, or he may be frightened by loud noises or a thunderstorm. A night-light in the bedroom helps to banish fear of the dark. And although you may often have to go into your child's bedroom to reassure him with calming words or a gentle back rub, at other times he may settle back to sleep after you call out to let him know you're in the next room or on your way to comfort him.

ONE TO THREE YEARS

Toddlers sleep about 10 to 13 hours out of the 24. However, children at the toddler stage are curious and contrary by nature. Once they can climb out of their cribs or beds, they may also seem to be convinced that there's a party going on somewhere in the house and want to join in the fun. Many parents go through a difficult phase of trying to keep their toddler in bed, especially around the time he switches to a regular bed. The best way to deal with this exasperating phase is to respond calmly to reasonable requests (such as for a drink of water), let your toddler see that

FREQUENT WAKINGS AT SIX MONTHS

If your 6-month-old baby regularly wakes up several times during the night, bring it to your pediatrician's attention.

nothing special is going on, and return him gently but firmly to bed each time he pops out.

Most toddlers still have an afternoon nap. But even when a child does not sleep, it's still a good idea to have a quiet period, perhaps with time to read a story in the early afternoon. This pattern may continue well into the preschool years; preschools and kindergartens usually have a rest period sometime during the school day.

Teething (also see p. 178) sometimes interferes with toddlers' sleep, as do colds and upper respiratory infections, which are especially common at this age. Many toddlers begin to recount vivid dreams almost as soon as they can string a simple sentence together, and nightmares are particularly scary to a young child who may not yet be able to draw a line between the real world and his imagination (also see Chapter 7). Nightmares may follow an upsetting event, such as a bad fall or a parent's angry outburst. Bad dreams are not usually a sign of trouble, but if they occur frequently enough to make you concerned, or your child's sleep

Growth is dependent on the interplay of several hormones. The main one is growth hormone, which is secreted by the pituitary gland. Although growth hormone is secreted during the day, the highest blood levels occur while children are sleeping at night. All children need adequate sleep to grow properly and, at every age, children need more sleep than adults. Youngsters need extra sleep during the massive growth spurts that take place during infancy and adolescence. It does not follow, however, that a child's growth will be stunted if she sleeps less than others her age, or that a child who sleeps a lot will be tall. Children's height is programmed in the genes they inherit. What's important, therefore, is that each child gets as much sleep as she needs to keep up a satisfactory rate of growth and a good level of activity.

is often broken up by nightmares, talk it over with your pediatrician. (Also see Chapter 8.)

Keeping to a regular bedtime makes it easier to cope with occasional exceptions to the schedule. When bedtime is delayed, settle your child with a shorter version of the usual going-to-bed routine.

Preschool Sleep Time

The typical resistance and orneriness of the toddler may give way to a period of sweet reasonableness at around age 3. In general, however, the preschool years are marked by phases of calm behavior alternating with periods of intense experimentation and even rebellion. Testing the limits with parents, caregivers, and daily routines such as eating, dressing, and going to bed allows the 3-year-old to gauge his position in the family and the degree to which he can control his environment. It's all part of his long drive to become an independent person.

Sleep deprivation is rarely seen in children younger than school age, because most have the ability to fall asleep almost anywhere and at any time to make up for missed nighttime sleep. If there's a problem at this age, it's more likely to be one of scheduling: a child who sleeps too long during the day and stays awake late at night, or whose sleeptime is otherwise out of sync with that of the rest of the family.

Preschoolers by and large are busy and active all day long. Most give up their daytime naps as they approach age 5. Some need an earlier bedtime when they first stop napping. And although some may try resistance or delaying tactics at bedtime, most will sleep for 10 to 12 hours a night. For the great majority, nighttime wakings are unusual. This is the time, however, when sleep disturbances such as sleepwalking and sleep terrors (see p. 151) are likely to appear in susceptible youngsters.

School Years

At age 5, some children still need a daytime nap to recharge their batteries, but most have learned to pace their activities throughout the day and sleep longer at night. As at every stage of childhood, it's best to keep to a routine without being rigid. In other words, if your child is tired or irritable during the day or wants to nap, let him do so. By the time they enter kindergarten, most children need 10 to 12 hours of sleep. If your child is getting to sleep late because her preschool or kindergarten insists on a daytime nap, ask if she may simply have a rest period without napping—perhaps quietly looking at a book, instead.

After a day of nonstop activities at school, the average 5-year-old is tired. Even if she resists the idea of going to sleep, it's a good idea to get her ready by giving her a bath and changing her into sleepwear for a quiet time—playing a board game, reading a story, or just talking over the events of the day—so that when the eyelids droop, it's only a step into bed (see Chapter 6).

The amount of sleep a school-age child needs decreases a little each year. It also varies from child to child depending on the level of physical activity and the individual temperament. The parents' activities also influence children's sleep. For example, parents who work on different shifts may have difficulty coordinating their schedules, with the result that the child's sleep is interrupted. Parents may not agree on the child's schedule: One wants to get the child to bed early, the other wants to spend some playtime with the child each night on returning late from work. Sometimes, a teacher is the first to notice that a child needs more sleep than he is actually getting. Children who regularly droop over their desks are often those who plead to stay up for "just one more" TV program or for the return home of a parent who regularly works late. Children need their sleep on school nights; perhaps adjustments can be made on weekends to allow for more companionable time together with the parent whom they usually see less during weekdays.

ADHD AND SLEEP

Parents of children with attention deficit hyperactivity disorder (ADHD) often complain that their children sleep less than others. However, studies comparing groups of youngsters with and without ADHD have not borne out this claim. When their sleeping habits were followed, youngsters with ADHD tended to wake more often during the night, but there was no difference between the groups in terms of the total time spent sleeping or the length of time required to fall asleep.

Responses to a questionnaire completed by the parents of almost a thousand grade-school children disclosed that bedtime resistance was the most common sleep-related problem: 27 percent of the children regularly put up a struggle against going to bed. Other common problems were trouble getting to sleep (11 percent), and trouble with morning waking and daytime tiredness (17 percent each). Waking up at night was the least common complaint, occurring in only 6 percent of children.

Many parents reported overlap between problems. For example, of the children who had trouble getting to sleep, 80 percent also put up resistance at bedtime, while 34 percent of those who resisted going to bed also had trouble getting to sleep. Parents who disliked dealing with bedtime resistance were likely to give in and let children go to bed later or fall asleep away from their beds. This inconsistent response only added to the problem, shifting the children's sleep phase (hours out of the 24 devoted to sleeping) progressively later and reinforcing the resistant behavior.

By age 11 or 12, youngsters need 10 hours of sleep a day. During the school week, they may have to be nudged to bed to make sure they get enough rest to keep up a busy schedule of schoolwork, sports, and extracurricular activities. However, a child may be allowed a bit more leeway with weekend bedtimes, depending on the activities planned for the next day.

SLEEPY ADOLESCENTS

With the onset of the adolescent growth spurt, teenagers' sleep patterns change (also see p. 187). Researchers who tracked links between adolescent sleep, school performance, and driving performance found that teenagers need, on average, 9.2 hours of sleep a night. However, the hormonal surges of puberty reset the adolescent body clock in such a way that youngsters may not only feel sleepy progressively later but may also be inclined to wake later as adolescence proceeds. In one study, high school freshmen slept on average 40 minutes longer each night than seniors. And all students tended to go to bed about 2 hours later, and to wake up about $3^1/_2$ hours later, on weekends.

School grades were a reliable indicator of the hours spent sleeping. Students whose report cards showed mainly As and Bs were the same youngsters who usually went to bed earlier on both school nights and weekends. These high achievers averaged about 35 more minutes of sleep nightly than those who got mostly Ds and Fs. At all ages, adolescents who got the most sleep, and who went to bed at about the same time on school nights and weekends, were more alert all day long. Those who slept less and had erratic bedtimes were not only drowsy during the day but were also more likely to be depressed.

If you answer "yes" to any of these questions, it may be time to bring the problem to your pediatrician's attention:

- Is my child difficult to wake up most mornings?

- Is my child lacking in energy?

- Does my child refuse meals because he's too tired to eat?

- Does my child have difficulty settling to sleep because she is overstimulated?

- Is my child often irritable or cranky at about the same time of the day?

- Have teachers reported that my child has trouble staying alert or paying attention in school?

- Are our family's nights disturbed because of our child's nighttime wakings?

The study echoed the 1925 landmark survey by Dr. Lewis Terman, originator of the Stanford-Binet Intelligence Test, which is still the most widely used to evaluate children's general intelligence. When Dr. Terman compared sleep habits in large groups of children who had IQs either higher than or lower than 140, he found that brighter youngsters tended to sleep longer, and that the longer children slept, the better they performed in school. Later studies in Japanese and Canadian children and in identical twins have borne out his observation: Brighter children generally get more sleep and the amount of sleep appears to be directly tied to school performance.

Sleepiness does more than drag down grades: Several studies have also shown that teenagers who don't sleep enough have a higher rate of car crashes (see p. 191). So compelling is the evidence linking adolescents' sleep and daytime performance that several school boards, responding to demands by doctors and parents, have set high school opening times an hour or more later in the hope that youngsters will get the extra sleep they need.

PARENTS NEED SLEEP, TOO

Try not to feel let down when you're still waking frequently even after your baby starts sleeping through the night. The reason is that your body needs time to readjust and settle back into its former sleeping patterns. However, if you had sleep troubles before your baby came on the scene, it's likely that the same problems will reappear or continue.

Lack of sleep affects every aspect of our functioning—not least, the way we function as parents. Those whose babies are poor sleepers tend to be more anxious and depressed, and to be less happy in their marriages. Conversely, when their baby sleeps well, parents are less anxious and depressed and express greater satisfaction with their marriages. Our memory is better and we perform job-related duties better when we sleep well. Fatigue due to lack of sleep is a leading cause of road crashes, causing injuries and fatalities everywhere in the world.

Adults need on average 8 hours of sleep a night. Some get by on about 7, while others perform best after 9 or 10 hours. Those who get less than 7 hours, however, are almost always sleep deprived. People who are sleep deprived look and feel washed out, and tend to get drowsy at odd times throughout the day. Evaluated under laboratory conditions, their sleep patterns differ according to whether they are sleep deprived or well rested.

Sleep is important throughout life, and not only when your child is an infant. If household tasks are keeping you up past your bedtime, try to deal with the most pressing ones and schedule the others at times that won't interfere with your rest. Perhaps you could farm out some of the chores at a modest cost. Or your children may be mature enough to take on regular chores and possibly to trade extra help for an allowance. If naps refresh you (some people feel groggy rather than well rested after a nap), time regular naps to fit in with your child's schedule. Take care that naps don't interfere with your nighttime sleep. If you usually have trouble falling asleep or have an irregular sleep/wake cycle, naps may not be a solution for you.

Keep to a regular schedule for going to bed and waking up, even on weekends. Sleeping late on weekends doesn't make up for sleep lost during the week. Avoid caffeine if it keeps you awake, and alcohol, which may make you sleepy at first but can cause wakefulness later in the night. Ask your physician's advice about sleep problems.

Many commonly used medications are known to influence the quality and quantity of our sleep. They include antidepressants, antihistamines, decongestants, and cough and cold remedies. Some women are surprised to find that sleep troubles disappear when they switch from oral contraceptive pills to other forms of birth control. Even sleeping pills, muscle relaxants, and sedatives can cause sleep difficulties. Although such medications may originally have been prescribed for reasons unrelated to sleep, eventually the body comes to depend on them and, in time, the user find it difficult to get to sleep without them. Avoid nonprescription sleeping remedies, which can have a rebound effect and make your sleep troubles worse.

Sleep experts caution that any substance that affects the nervous system is likely to have an effect on our sleep. Nicotine, a stimulant drug, is one example. Even though you may be a non-smoker, smoke from others' cigarettes may make it hard for you to get to sleep after a social event and leave you feeling poorly rested and hung-over the next morning.

Anxiety and depression commonly interfere with sleep in two ways. In a depressed or anxious state we may find it difficult to fall asleep or we may wake up with a start and remain wide-eyed and anxious through the early morning hours. Either way, the anxious person doesn't sleep enough, feels exhausted during the day, and may face each succeeding night with increasing anxiety about not getting the sleep he or she needs. And although insomnia often occurs with emotional upset, depression can also lead a person to sleep many more hours than usual and wake up feeling groggy, tired—and still depressed.

If you have physical or emotional problems that are interfering with your sleep—or even if you don't have any problems and you still can't sleep—schedule an appointment with your doctor, who will be able to suggest behavioral and lifestyle measures and may prescribe a short course of medication. When sleep troubles are deep-seated, your doctor may recommend consultation with another specialist.

CHAPTER 3

The First Few Months

I t's understandable that so many new parents become obsessed with sleep—not only their own, but also that of their infants. As one mother put it: "When my baby's asleep, I'm constantly checking her to make sure she's breathing and okay. When I'm trying to get some sleep myself, that's when she's wide awake and wants to eat, or be changed, or just have my attention. I now understand the real meaning of sleep deprivation!" Little wonder that a baby's sleeping through the night becomes a major milestone—at least for the parents.

Without any prompting from their parents, newborn babies get all the sleep they need. When they are not being fed or otherwise tended to, very young infants are likely to be asleep. Undoubtedly, the term "sleeps like a baby" refers to the newborn's innate ability to fall asleep at any time and in any place. But when it comes to the parents' getting a good night's sleep, the first few weeks of parenthood are rough indeed.

Chronic sleep deprivation exacts a tremendous emotional as well as physical toll. Some doctors believe that the prolonged depression that some new mothers experience is, at least in part, tied to a lack of sleep in the early weeks of caring for a newborn.

Babies don't need to be taught how to sleep. Like the other vital functions, it just comes naturally. But good sleep habits are something else. They must be learned and nurtured, and the earlier the better.

As the baby begins to sleep for longer periods each night, the depression typically lifts. In any event, chronic lack of sleep can try the patience of even the most devoted and loving parents. In the minds of many, an "easy" baby is defined as one whose sleep patterns allow the parents to get enough sleep themselves. Thus, there is all the more reason to help your baby establish healthy sleep habits in the first few months of life.

THE NEWBORN PERIOD

A baby's sleep/wake cycle begins to develop before birth, and by the time the fetus reaches full term, about 60 percent of his time is spent sleeping, or in a sleeplike state. During the first few weeks of life, babies typically sleep most of the time—16 to 17 hours a day. But their sleep is usually in short takes. They wake up every 2 to 4 hours—day and night—needing to be fed, changed, and tended to. For parents, who are used to doing most of their sleeping in a single stretch at night, this is indeed an exhausting time.

Happily, relief is in sight. At 4 weeks of age, most babies begin

SWITCH TO BABY TIME

As much as possible, go on "baby time" for the first few weeks or even months. Catch a nap when your baby is sleeping and, for the time being, forget about trying to do all your sleeping in a single nighttime stretch. Save your energy for getting to know and enjoy your new baby.

You may be lucky enough to have a family member or paid help to pitch in with laundry, housework, and other chores. If not, perhaps you could work out a system with other new parents in your neighborhood, trading off baby-sitting, food shopping, and household tasks. In this way, each member of the "cooperative" could count on an uninterrupted stretch of time two or three times a week for napping or catching up on chores. Another possibility might be to hire a high school or college student as a mother's helper for a few hours each week.

Sleep patterns in newborn infants are different from those in older children and adults (see Chapter 1). Sleep in newborn babies is about equally divided between rapid eye movement (REM) and non-REM sleep, and follows these stages:

Stage 1. Drowsiness, in which the baby starts to fall asleep.

Stage 2. REM sleep (also referred to as "active sleep"), in which the baby may twitch or jerk his arms or legs, and his eyes move under his closed eyelids. Breathing is often irregular and may stop for 5 to 10 seconds—a condition called normal periodic breathing of infancy—and then start again with a burst of rapid breathing at the rate of 50 to 60 breaths a minute for 10 to 15 seconds, followed by regular breathing until the cycle repeats itself. The baby's skin color does not change with the pauses in breathing and there is no cause for concern (in contrast to apnea, see pp. 42–43). Babies generally outgrow periodic breathing by about the middle of the first year.

Stage 3. Light sleep, in which breathing becomes more regular, and sleep becomes less active.

Stages 4 and 5. Deep non-REM sleep (also referred to as quiet sleep). Twitching and other movement cease, and the baby falls into sleep that becomes progressively deeper. During these stages, the baby is very difficult to waken.

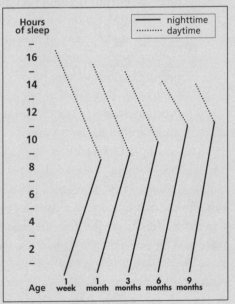

sleeping for somewhat longer periods during the night, with a longer period of wakefulness during the early evening. Between 4 and 6 weeks of age, sleep begins to consolidate even more in relation to daylight and darkness. In effect, circadian rhythms (see *Biological Clocks*, p. 6) are being established. After 2 or 3 months, healthy babies usually settle into a routine in which they sleep for longer stretches at night—say, 5 or more hours—and are awake and active more during the day, with three or four daytime naps. By the age of 6 months, almost all babies should be able to sleep through the night, and by 9 months, most take only two daytime naps. There is, however, a big difference between the average and what really happens in any given family. Pediatricians report that issues concerning sleep are near the top of any list of parental concerns:

> "Timmy is now 8 months old, and he still gets us up two or three times every night. It may take an hour or more to get him back to sleep."
>
> "Every night it takes me hours to get Shawna settled down enough to stay in bed, and by then I'm totally worn out!"
>
> "Kelly can't get to sleep unless I'm rocking her. I've tried shutting the door and letting her cry herself to sleep, but after several minutes of listening to her sobbing, I can't stand it anymore, and I end up rocking her for the next hour."
>
> "Kenny may be worn out, but he still drags out the bedtime ritual. It's just one more story, song, glass of water, trip to the bathroom..."

Granted, some lucky parents escape such traps. Between the ages of 3 and 6 months, their babies naturally seem to fall into a happy routine: They go to bed with nary a whimper, sleep through the night, and take a couple of lengthy naps during the day. When they are awake, they are cheerful and alert. Of course, there may be restless nights when the baby is fussy or sick, but these are the exception rather than the rule, and the baby soon returns to his normal routine.

For all too many parents, however, this sounds like an

An Infant Who Won't Sleep Alone

 Our 2-month-old won't sleep in his own bed. He has slept with us since his birth. We've tried lullabies, talking to him, and letting him cry, but he will only sleep in our arms.

Your infant can learn to sleep where you put him to sleep, but it takes patience and perseverance. Follow a regular bedtime routine, then put your baby in his crib still awake, and return at intervals to reassure him (also see p. 37).

impossible dream. But it needn't be that way. Good sleep habits can be instilled almost from the very beginning. You may need to experiment a bit, but in general, here's how to begin, even before your baby is ready to sleep for more than a few hours at a time.

1. Start by helping "set" the sleep/wake cycle of your baby's inborn biological clock. As noted in Chapter 1, this internal clock takes important cues from the outside world. Your goal is to have the sleep cycle coincide with nighttime. Many new

Forming Sleep Associations

 How can I teach my baby (7 months) to go to sleep without a bottle?

Make sure your baby's nutritional needs are met at her scheduled feedings and then help her form comfortable sleep associations (see p. 78). If she needs to suck for comfort, she may accept a pacifier or learn to suck her thumb. Babies should never be given bottles in bed; this practice can harm the developing teeth and possibly increase the risk of ear infections. A transitional object may be comforting.

mothers insist that rooming-in at the hospital—in which they keep their babies in their own quiet, darkened room rather than in a brightly lit hospital nursery—makes a difference, even though it's only for a night or two. If rooming-in is not possible, you can start the readjustment as soon as you take your baby home. During the day, open the blinds to let daylight in or turn on the lights in the baby's room, even when he is sleeping.

2. Expose the baby to normal levels of daytime noise. Don't feel you have to whisper and tiptoe around. When a baby is tired, she'll sleep through a normal amount of noise. But if she becomes used to a super-quiet environment, she may become overly sensitive to noise, and every little nighttime sound will waken her.

3. During the day, encourage your baby to stay awake for longer periods. Use this time to cuddle, play with, and get to know your baby. If he spends most of the day sleeping and is awake most of the night, try to reverse the pattern by waking him to eat and play during the day.

4. As evening approaches, switch to a dimmer and quieter environment. Spend less time playing and giving extra attention. Put your baby to sleep in a darkened, quiet room. Your baby is still likely to wake up every 2 or 3 hours, but given the right environmental cues, this should begin to change in a few weeks. Your baby will be more awake and active during the day, and the nighttime sleep periods will become a bit longer. By 6 to 8 weeks, some babies start skipping one of the nighttime feedings.

THE NEXT PHASE

Some babies naturally start to sleep through the night—or at least for a stretch of 5 or 6 hours—when they are 6 to 12 weeks old. More often, however, parents have to give them a bit of a nudge by teaching them to fall asleep on their own. This is important because babies—like older children and adults—go through several periods of arousal and waking during the night. A baby

SWADDLING CAN HELP AN INFANT SLEEP

My 6-week-old infant thrashes about and cries out when he sleeps. He continually hits himself in the face and wakes up. Is this behavior normal? How do I help him to sleep better?

Many infants move about and whimper in their sleep. They sometimes wake themselves because they cannot yet control the movements of their hands and arms.

One way to help your baby, until he has better motor control, is by swaddling; that is, wrap him from the shoulders down in a sheet or a lightweight receiving blanket. Some babies sleep well if they are swaddled firmly; others seem to prefer a lighter wrap that lets them keep their arms partly free. An infant may also sleep better if, in addition to being swaddled, he is placed on his back with his head and body braced against the end and side of the crib and cushioned by the bumper. Even tiny infants may wriggle about until they squeeze themselves into this position, as if to recapture the cozy surroundings they were used to up until birth. As your baby develops more motor control, he will need less swaddling.

who knows how to comfort herself is likely to go back to sleep in a few minutes. **Babies learn this by being put in their cribs while still awake.**

A newborn often falls fast asleep while feeding or being rocked, and does not wake up when being put in his bed. But after the newborn phase—at about 6 to 8 weeks of age—it's time for your baby to start learning how to go to sleep on his own. Instead of rocking a baby to sleep or allowing him to doze off while feeding, you should keep your baby awake: Sing or talk to your baby in a soft voice, stroke his head, play with his feet. Let him get groggy

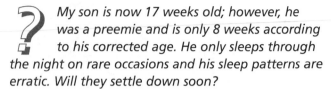

Sleep Patterns in a Premature Baby

My son is now 17 weeks old; however, he was a preemie and is only 8 weeks according to his corrected age. He only sleeps through the night on rare occasions and his sleep patterns are erratic. Will they settle down soon?

Premature babies tend to wake more often at night than full-term infants, at least for the first several months. Night-waking and lighter sleep are part of a survival and developmental mechanism that protects preemies. Their systems for breathing and circulation are under the control of a nervous system that is not yet mature. This keeps a premature baby in a state in which he is more easily aroused for feeding. Preemies spend more of their sleeptime in REM sleep, and child development specialists believe that this may be part of a mechanism that helps the brain develop normally. Your baby will settle in time, but you should be prepared for frequent night-waking during the next few months.

or drowsy, and then put him into bed on his back (see *Back to Sleep*, p. 44). At first, he may become more awake and fuss or even cry. Draw the shades or turn down the lights, tell him good night in a soft, loving voice, and leave the room. You might want to place a small, soft toy in the crib where he can see it.

Even if he begins to wail, resist going back in for a few minutes. If the crying continues, go to the crib, pat him gently in a soothing manner, but don't pick him up. After he calms down, again leave the room. If he continues to cry, wait a few minutes longer than the last time, then repeat the soothing visit. It may take a few days, but eventually, your baby will learn to fall asleep in his crib on his own.

Some babies learn to put themselves to sleep with the help of

THE SOLID FOOD MYTH

? *My baby is almost 3 months old, and still wakes up hungry at least once or twice during the night. My mother insists that I could solve the problem by giving him some cereal in the evening. However, my pediatrician says wait another couple of months before starting solid foods. Who's right?*

Follow your pediatrician's advice. Your mother's generation tended to introduce solid foods earlier than pediatricians now recommend. Even so, there's no relationship between starting solid foods and sleeping through the night. Many babies start sleeping through the night before starting solid foods, while others still want a nighttime feeding even though they are eating solid foods during the day.

a soothing sensation, such as rocking themselves or sucking a thumb or a hand. Others want to feel a soft toy or lightweight blanket. Go with whatever works and is safe. However, never put your baby to bed with a bottle for comfort. The natural sugar in many liquids promotes the growth of the bacteria that cause tooth decay and the effect is especially severe when the sugary residue stays in the mouth all night long. This can result in serious dental decay, known as "nursing bottle caries" in the developing primary teeth. Liquid, even water, pooling in the mouth can also back up through the eustachian tubes, the tiny passages that run between the throat and the ear. This sets up conditions that foster the development of ear infections.

WAKING DURING THE NIGHT

A baby who is 3 or 4 months old should be able to sleep for a long stretch—say 5 or 6 hours—during the night. But he may wake up

Breast vs. Bottle

? *My sister's baby, who is bottle fed, started sleeping through the night when he was barely 3 months old. My breastfed baby is 2 months older, and still wants to be fed two or three times during the night. My sister says breastfed babies are slower to sleep through the night than those who are bottle fed. Is this true?*

Although there are many exceptions, breastfed babies generally do want more frequent feedings—including during the night—for a longer period than babies who are fed formula. Some experts attribute this to the fact that breastmilk is easier and faster to digest than formula. Thus, a meal of breastmilk may be digested in 2 or 3 hours, and the baby will be ready to feed again. Also, breastfed babies who fall asleep while feeding may have difficulty getting back to sleep unless they are allowed to nurse. To encourage your baby to start sleeping through the night, try changing your nighttime responses. Don't rush in at the first whimper; instead, wait a few minutes to see if your baby will fall back to sleep. And don't let her fall asleep while nursing. Instead, put her in the crib drowsy but awake, and let her fall asleep on her own.

The American Academy of Pediatrics encourages mothers to breastfeed exclusively for the first 6 months, and to continue breastfeeding for at least 12 months or as long as baby and mother want to continue. (See also p. 87.)

every couple of hours. Don't rush to the crib every time you hear your baby whimper—wait a few minutes and see if he'll fall back asleep without attention. But if your baby's cry is one of distress or it persists for more than a few minutes, by all means go to him.

Perhaps it's a holdover from the Puritan past or—farther back—the caveman's fear of wild beasts lurking beyond the firelight. Whatever the reason may be, some people persist in putting a moralistic slant on infants' vital functions and behavior: "He's been *bad* today, he wouldn't finish his bottle," "She was *good* for a change, she slept through the night," or "She was *really bad*, she yelled and wriggled when I was trying to change her diaper."

Little babies may be happy or sad, confident or fearful, hungry or satisfied—but they are never bad, and they only want to please you, their parents. Your child will learn to be a good, kind, ethical, and self-controlled person from the example you set day in, day out. Her vital functions—such as eating and sleeping—and her social skills—including learning to use the toilet and staying dry at night—are a neutral zone. They are essential to your child's happiness and sense of well-being, but they are not tools for teaching right from wrong.

Avoid turning on the light if possible. Check whether he needs changing; if so, try to change the diaper without picking your baby up. After he calms down, say good night in a soft voice, and leave the room. A baby who has learned to put himself to sleep will probably doze off in a few minutes.

SPECIAL SITUATIONS

Breastfed babies typically start sleeping through the night somewhat later than those who are bottle fed and they may need a nighttime feeding for longer. But by age 5 or 6 months, they, too, should sleep through most of the night (see *Breast vs. Bottle*, opposite page).

Premature babies also take longer to sleep through the night. A baby who is born 6 weeks before term, for example, may take an extra 6 or 7 weeks to reach this milestone. Although it may take longer to achieve the ultimate goal, you still should work on instilling good sleep habits by putting the baby to bed while he is still awake, and helping him learn to go to sleep on his own.

VIVE LA DIFFÉRENCE

Remember, no two babies are exactly alike, especially when it comes to establishing a sleep/wake schedule. Some are sleeping through the night at 6 weeks; others don't reach this landmark until 6 months. And some babies are just naturally little night owls. In fact, this pattern may be apparent even before birth. Many mothers of babies who want to sleep during the day and be awake and active at night report that a similar pattern prevailed during pregnancy. And in some, the pattern persists throughout childhood and into adult life. This doesn't necessarily mean that there's nothing you can do to alter the pattern, but it is important to get to know your baby, and to work out a sleep schedule that feels best for all involved.

PERIODIC BREATHING VS. APNEA IN INFANTS

New parents are often alarmed when they notice that their baby momentarily stops breathing while sleeping. Pauses may last for about 10 seconds at a time, then breathing starts again at a faster rate for about 15 to 20 seconds, followed by regular breaths until the cycle recurs.

A baby's respiratory system develops after birth; before that, the fetus takes oxygen from the mother's blood. Immediately after being born, the baby gasps and inhales air, which inflates the lungs. But although the baby "practices" breathing before birth by making rhythmic movements that strengthen the muscles between the ribs, it takes a while for breathing muscles and responses to develop fully. Thus, every now and then, breathing stops altogether. This is referred to as periodic breathing of infancy and is a normal stage of development. It does not indicate that the airway is blocked. Periodic breathing is most pronounced during REM sleep. In part, this is because the activity of all muscles—including the muscles that control the rib cage—is inhibited during REM sleep.

APNEA. While periodic breathing is a normal developmental stage, apnea—pauses in breathing accompanied by changes in the heart, blood circulation, and nervous system—can adversely affect the baby and, in some cases, may warn that the baby has an increased risk of SIDS (sudden infant death syndrome). If your baby has prolonged (more than 10 seconds) pauses in breathing or has bluish skin, a fever, or other symptoms of illness, call the Emergency Medical Service or your pediatrician at once.

OBSTRUCTIVE/MIXED APNEA. As its name implies, obstructive apnea occurs when the airway is partially blocked (also see p. 60). The term mixed apnea refers to temporary halts in breathing due to obstruction in the upper airway as well as factors under the control of the central nervous system. In young infants, apnea may occur as the chest muscles involved in breathing become tired. The airways may be obstructed by a buildup of mucus or by a suppression of cough reflexes during sleep. Other factors that increase the occurrence of obstructive apnea include relaxation of the muscles (which include those of the mouth cavity and throat) during REM sleep, respiratory infection, blockage in the nose, malformation of the face or head, flexion of the neck, and lack of sleep. Apnea is also common in babies who are exposed to secondhand tobacco smoke, even before birth.

Although most sleep apneas are harmless and disappear as the

S My Baby Breathing Normally?

Healthy infants take from 20 to 60 breaths a minute. Breathing rates are normally quite irregular and it's not unusual for a baby to pause for up to 10 seconds without taking a breath. This breathing pattern gradually disappears by the time the baby is about 6 months old. It is perfectly normal but can be a heart-stopping event for new parents who are not prepared for it. If your baby stops breathing for longer than 10 seconds, call the Emergency Medical Service or your pediatrician.

baby matures or the underlying condition is treated, there are exceptions. Prolonged apneas may be a forerunner of sudden infant death syndrome (see following section). Babies with a history of serious episodes of sleep apnea—for example, prolonged cessation of breathing that requires resuscitation—require medical investigation and, if appropriate, treatment. A crib monitor may also be recommended for such children. This is a device that sounds an alarm if breathing stops for a predetermined number of seconds. However, for babies who are healthy and who merely have the typical "stop and start" periodic breathing of infancy, crib monitors are not necessary. Contrary to the exaggerated claims of some marketers, these devices do not help prevent SIDS in normally healthy children, and may only increase anxiety in parents who have nothing to worry about. (For a discussion of sleep apnea in older children, see Chapter 4.)

Preventing SIDS

BACK TO SLEEP. Doctors don't know what causes SIDS; in all probability, there are several different causes. However, pediatricians in several countries, including the United States, have found that the number of deaths from SIDS can be cut by up to half when babies are *not* placed in the tummy-down position to sleep. And there are additional measures you can take to keep your baby safer.

Put your baby to sleep on her back, with her feet against the footboard of the crib. If she tends to push herself into a side position, make sure her lower arm is extended forward, to prevent her from rolling on to her stomach. Pediatricians may recommend that babies who spit up a lot be laid to sleep on the right side. This helps prevent excessive spitting up, because the stomach fills from the left and empties on the right. Show grandparents, home helpers, and anyone else who will be looking after your child the correct way to position her. (They may tell you that their babies slept fine on their tummies. If so, tell them you understand, but that your baby sleeps her own way, on her back.)

While it's important to position your baby on her back for

sleep, she should have plenty of tummy time down on the floor when you are playing with her. This is necessary to help her strengthen her upper body and arms and develop her motor skills.

BEDDING. To eliminate the risk of SIDS through suffocation due to soft bedding, the American Academy of Pediatrics, the U.S. Consumer Product Safety Commission, and the National Institute of Child Health and Human Development have revised their recommendations for putting infants down to sleep. These

SLEEPING POSITION AND HEAD SHAPE

A baby who always sleeps with her head in the same position may rub a bald spot or develop flattening on one side of the skull. Neither condition is harmful; however, it can be prevented by alternating the way you place her in the crib. Babies tend to turn their heads in the direction of the most activity, such as toward the door. Therefore, placing your baby a different way every few nights will vary the position of her head. Also, during the day, change your baby's position from time to time, and let her spend some time propped up in an infant seat. As your baby becomes strong enough to change her head position, the head will become rounded again and new hair will grow to cover up the bald spot.

organizations recommend that infants under 12 months be put to sleep in a crib with no soft bedding of any kind. They suggest that parents use one-piece sleepers or other sleep clothing, with no other covering, as an alternative to blankets. If you use a thin blanket, tuck it around the crib mattress, reaching only as far as your baby's chest, to reduce the risk of getting her head covered by the bedding.

Fit your baby's crib with a firm mattress and make sure there's no space between the mattress and the crib walls. Your baby should never sleep on a water bed, sheepskin, pillow, sofa, or

HOW LONG SHOULD BABIES SLEEP ON THEIR BACKS?

 Now that my 5-month-old baby is rolling over by himself, is it safe to let him sleep on his tummy? If not, what is the best way to keep him on his back?

The American Academy of Pediatrics recommends that parents place healthy infants on their backs to sleep, to reduce the risk of sudden infant death syndrome (SIDS). The number of cases of SIDS has been cut in half since babies have been placed on their backs, instead of their stomachs, for sleeping.

We don't know exactly how long babies should sleep on their backs; however, once a baby can roll over (this generally happens between 4 and 7 months), he's usually past the highest-risk time for SIDS. There's probably no need to roll him onto his back or prevent him from changing position.

other soft surface. Thick blankets, duvets, comforters, pillows, and large, soft, stuffed toys should never be used in babies' cribs; a baby can easily be smothered if trapped under bulky bedding or when her face is pressed up against a pillow.

Babies do not need extra support, such as from rolled blankets or commercial devices, to keep them on their backs. Cumbersome materials like these clutter up the crib and may be hazardous for an infant.

TEMPERATURE. Babies should be kept warm, but they shouldn't get overheated. Make sure the crib isn't standing next to a radiator, which can quickly heat up the bedding. And keep the temperature of the room comfortable and on the cool side: between 65° and 70°F is ideal.

SLEEPWEAR. Dress your baby in about as many layers as you wear. At night, change your baby out of day clothes and into flame-retardant sleepwear. Many parents prefer to dress their infants in an all-in-one sleeper that can be zipped up. This keeps the baby comfortably warm and does away with the need for covers. This eliminates the risk—admittedly small—of the baby's becoming tangled and smothering under blankets.

BREASTFEEDING. The American Academy of Pediatrics encourages mothers to breastfeed exclusively for the first 6 months (about the time your baby's diet begins to include solid foods) and to continue breastfeeding for at least 12 months or as long as baby and mother want to continue. (See also p. 87.) Breastmilk is the ideal food for infants. It also provides antibodies that help protect children against infections until their own immune systems are mature enough to take over this essential function.

THE QUESTION OF CRYING

Typically, newborns and young babies cry an average of $2^1/2$ to 3 hours a day. While it's normal for babies to cry, it's also normal for parents to want the crying to stop. But it's important to realize that crying is a baby's major means of communication, and that not every cry is a sign of hunger or distress. Granted, babies cry when they are hungry, in pain, or need changing, but they also cry when they are bored, overstimulated, annoyed, or simply want attention. It doesn't take parents long to be able to interpret their baby's cries, and to respond appropriately.

Colic is another matter. Without a doubt, parents find infant colic the most frustrating and difficult form of crying. Incon-

NO-SMOKING ZONE

Create a smoke-free zone around your baby. Infants and young children exposed to tobacco smoke have more colds and upper respiratory infections, as well as a higher risk of sudden infant death syndrome (SIDS). The risk of SIDS is higher for babies whose mothers smoked during pregnancy. No one should smoke in your house or car, or anywhere around your baby.

Your child's bedroom and crib or bed should be extra safe. Her crib and—once she's mobile—her room are where she will first push the boundaries of exploration, without direct supervision much of the time. To keep the path clear, her surroundings should be free, as far as possible, of traps and hazards.

Check that all furniture complies with up-to-date safety requirements and is appropriate for your child's age. This is especially important when you are using previously owned pieces either bought or passed on as gifts. Antique cribs, for example, may look pretty, but the spacing between the slats rarely conforms to the current standard of $2^3/8$ inches or less, which is intended to make it impossible for a baby's head to become caught. In addition, the finish may include old layers of lead-based paint. You can trust new furniture if it bears the Juvenile Product Manufacturers' Association safety certification seal. All fabrics used in your child's room—sleepwear, sheets, curtains—should be flame retardant.

solable crying for hours at a time is the hallmark of infant colic. For the first few weeks of life, the baby follows a normal routine of crying for a definable reason, such as hunger or a need for changing. Then at about 3 or 4 weeks of age the baby starts crying for no apparent reason. Typically, the crying occurs at about the same time on most days, usually in the late afternoon or evening, and lasts for 3 or more hours at a time. The baby may pass gas or draw up her legs as if in pain. After several hours of wailing, the crying stops as abruptly as it began and the baby falls into a peaceful sleep. By that time, however, the parents are distraught, nervous wrecks.

Usually, the baby's pediatrician cannot find a physical cause for the crying. A number of theories as to what causes colic have been advanced—for example, allergies, an immature gastrointestinal

- Bars should be spaced no more than 2³/₈ inches apart.

- The mattress should be very firm and should not sag under your child's weight. It should fit snugly, with no space between it and the crib walls.

- The top of the crib rail should be at least 26 inches from the top of the mattress. Periodically lower the mattress as your child gets taller.

- The head- and foot-boards should be solid, with no decorative cutouts. Corner posts that could cause injury or snag clothing should be removed.

- Every time you put your baby in the crib, check that the side-rail release mechanism is locked and cannot be accidentally released. Never leave your baby in the crib when the side rail is lowered. (However, once an older toddler can climb in and out, it may be safer to make a bed with the mattress on the floor until you can get a new bed.)

- Crib bumpers help protect infants from drafts and bumps, but should be removed once your baby can pull herself up to a standing position. (For suggestions about padding a head banger's crib, see p. 157.)

- Keep large toys and stuffed animals out of the crib, as your baby may use them to get a leg up and over the rail. Pillows, bulky comforters, and heavy blankets do not belong in a crib; a baby can smother under them.

- Place the crib away from windows, where direct sunlight and drafts can make your child uncomfortable. A crib can become uncomfortably hot if placed too near a radiator.

- Once your child is about 3 feet tall, she should start sleeping in a bed.

TIPS ON COPING WITH COLIC

- Consult your pediatrician to rule out a medical cause for the colicky crying.

- Check to make sure that your baby is not in pain from a hair or thread wound around a toe, a finger, or even his penis; check that he doesn't have an arm or leg caught between the crib slats.

- If you are breastfeeding, ask your pediatrician about dietary changes. Occasionally, it helps to eliminate dairy products, caffeine, or gas-producing foods such as onions, cabbage, and beans. Commercial products can be used to reduce the gassiness associated with dried beans and legumes.

- Try swaddling your baby firmly in a light blanket or hold her close. Some colicky babies calm down when they feel warm and secure.

- Lay your baby on his tummy and gently rub his back. This can comfort a gassy baby. Place your baby on his back to sleep (see p. 44).

- Place your baby where he can hear a steady, rhythmic sound such as a clothes washer or dryer. (Never put your baby close to a heat source or on top of the machine. The baby could roll off or be jiggled off by the vibrations.)

system, overstimulation—but none have been proved. It's likely that a combination of factors are involved. Some experts say that in certain babies, colic may be a variation of normal behavior. Babies typically cry for 2¹/₂ to 3 hours over the course of a day, but a colicky baby may be doing all his crying at one stretch. In any event, about one in five babies develops colic; it is somewhat more common among first babies, and boys are affected more often than girls. Difficult as colic is, parents can take comfort in the fact that it rarely lasts beyond 4 or 5 months of age. (See box, *Tips on Coping with Colic.*)

- Quietly sing or hum a rhythmic tune. Or play soothing music at low volume.

- Some colicky babies are soothed by motion, such as rocking, being walked while in an infant carrier, riding in a car, or being placed in an infant swing.

- Take turns with your partner or get help to comfort your baby. A baby is quick to sense when a caregiver feels frustrated or upset, and he may respond by crying even harder.

- Try to take regular breaks. If you haven't yet found a dependable sitter, at least alternate evenings with your partner so that one of you can get out of the house for a short break.

- Prolonged crying can awaken feelings of anger and frustration. Admit to these, but if you feel yourself losing control and are fearful that you may harm your baby, immediately call your pediatrician, a parents' support group, or someone who can give you a break. Above all, **never shake your baby**. This can result in permanent brain damage and even death.

- Take comfort in the fact that difficult as it is, colic is a stage that lasts for only a few months.

CONSISTENCY, CONSISTENCY

Babies are fast learners, especially when it comes to getting their parents to respond to their wishes. Of course, you should heed your baby's demands for food, changing, and attention. And you should take time to cuddle—and savor getting to know—this marvelous little person. At the same time, you must help your baby learn good sleep habits as a prelude to other steps in self-discipline and self-reliance. This requires a consistent approach and establishing a set bedtime routine (see Chapter 6).

Remember, too, that there are no absolute rules that work for everyone; common sense must prevail. Find what seems to work best for your baby and you, and then stick to it. If your baby is teething or has a cold, you may need to alter the bedtime and naptime routines until the situation goes back to normal. A baby who is sick needs extra cuddling, care, and attention until his symptoms clear up and he feels well again. But then, return to the established routine. This way, the entire family can enjoy a good night's sleep!

CHAPTER 4

Problems in Sleeping Through the Night

A t every age, children's sleep patterns are influenced by interactions among developmental, biological, and emotional factors. For example, infants spend longer periods in active REM sleep (see p. 12) than older children and adults. Young babies generally don't have trouble falling asleep but, because REM sleep is associated with wakefulness, sleep disorders at this age for the most part are problems with staying asleep.

During the preschool and early school years, youngsters have recurrent, longer episodes of non-REM sleep with partial arousals—which occur during the transitions from non-REM to REM phases—throughout the night. The conditions known as parasomnias—sleepwalking, sleeptalking, sleep terrors (also see Chapter 8)— occur during partial arousals and, therefore, are prevalent in this age group. Some children have more frequent episodes of partial arousal during periods of emotional stress, such as family upheavals or school exams. Nightmares occur during REM sleep

Most nighttime wakings in childhood are not signs of sleep problems. Rather, they reflect stages in development and thus are keyed to successive age levels. Most are mild and transient, and do not require intervention by a health professional. Parents generally get through these phases with a little reassurance from their pediatrician.

and do not strictly belong among the events that occur with partial arousals. Nevertheless, they are common in these years and may also be triggered by stress and emotional trauma.

Adolescents have an increased need for sleep, which is partly tied to the hormonal changes driving the growth spurt (see Chapter 11). However, the desire to sleep may conflict with the pressures many teenagers feel to succeed in school, earn money with a part-time job, and spend time with their friends. The effect of such pressures is that many teenagers do not follow regular schedules for going to bed and waking up, thus disrupting their sleep/wake cycle and decreasing the overall time spent sleeping. The result is that teenagers' sleep problems mainly involve shifts in the sleep/wake cycle and the circadian rhythms.

Although nighttime disruptions are so frequent as to be considered part of normal development, sleep problems are also common, affecting up to 30 percent of all children at one time or another. Before puberty, the most frequent causes are health issues such as respiratory disorders and neurologic problems. Emotional stress brought on by family tensions, school problems, and psychological or psychiatric problems can also interfere with sleep. In adolescence, depression, anxiety, and problems with alcohol and/or drugs may play a role.

NIGHT WAKINGS IN THE FIRST YEAR

Somewhere around the middle of the first year, babies mature to a point where they can get through the night without a feeding and can soothe themselves back to sleep when they awaken but are not hungry or uncomfortable for some other reason.

If your baby wakes up and cries in obvious distress, attend to his needs promptly and gently, without a fuss. When the baby is calm and drowsy but still awake, put him back in his crib, say good night, and leave the room (also see Chapter 6). If your baby whimpers, don't rush back in. Instead, give him a few minutes to settle on his own. If the crying shows no sign of letting up and you can hear your baby becoming distressed, return briefly to comfort him. He may be feeling the first stirrings of separation anxiety and may need a little reassurance that you are nearby. Keep the room dim, try gently patting or rubbing him, but avoid picking him up if you can. When he is calm, leave the room again. Repeat the procedure, if necessary, at increasingly longer intervals but no more than about 10 minutes, until your baby settles back to sleep.

TODDLERS AND SCHOOL-AGE CHILDREN

TODDLERS. The surge of independence that accompanies your child's mastery of walking may be overtaken by a return to clinginess around 18 months of age. Psychologists have suggested that this stage may be a reaction to the toddler's growing awareness of separation. Attachment to transitional objects is more intense now than at any other stage. The teddy bear, blanket, or whatever the favorite may be is a stand-in for the parent or caregiver and helps the child make the crossover to symbolic thinking. In other words, when Mommy or Daddy is too busy to provide attention, the teddy bear is ready, willing, and able.

At around 2 years, the toddler's mixed feelings about her increasing independence lead to oppositional behavior, where a resounding "No!" is the usual response, sometimes accompanied by vigorous head nodding indicating her real wish to say "yes." Crying and emotional outbursts may be everyday events for a while. When your toddler flings herself on the floor, kicking and fighting, remind yourself that this is part of normal development and does not reflect badly on your ability as a parent. Try to keep toddler tantrums within limits by seeing that your child doesn't become overtired, overstimulated, or unnecessarily frustrated. Set reasonable guidelines for behavior. Children are more likely to have tantrums if parents are either too strict or fail to set any limits at all. This oppositional phase may stretch from about age 1 to 4 years. If tantrums persist after age 4, your pediatrician may recommend an evaluation. Parent education and support groups can also be helpful.

Toddlers are also creatures of habit. They thrive on routines— not only going-to-bed routines, but also regular schedules for

THAT'S ENTERTAINMENT!

Our 15-month-old is having terrible sleeping problems. He goes to bed around 9:00 P.M., wakes up at 1:00 A.M., and is wide awake until 4:00 A.M. Then he sleeps until 8:00 and stays up until his 1-hour afternoon nap. Thank goodness for Sesame Street *in the middle of the night!*

As long as you provide entertainment at night, your child will wake up for it. If the TV/VCR is in his room, move it out. Keep the bedroom dark, with only a night-light to orient your child. When he wakes up, comfort him but don't turn on the light, and speak no more than you have to. Tell him it's time to sleep and all the *Sesame Street* people are asleep, too. Make sure he has a cuddly toy—perhaps a *Sesame Street* character—or another transitional object to comfort himself with as he falls asleep. It may take some time for your toddler to learn a new sleep habit, but if you are consistent, he will sleep through the night and perhaps nap longer during the daytime in order to get the 10 to 12 hours' sleep that most children require at his age.

The American Academy of Pediatrics recommends that youngsters watch TV and videos (and when older, play computer games) for no more than 1 to 2 hours a day. The Academy recommends no TV or video watching at all for children under age 2.

For children who do watch TV and videos, there should be no viewing in the hour or so before bed, to help them sleep. It's not only scary programs that promote wakefulness; the lights, images, and sounds also stimulate the nervous system and can keep youngsters awake.

meals and snacks, going for walks, story time, and the hundred and one activities that fill their days. If a routine is disrupted, even a normally easy-going toddler may become upset. Keep to your regular routines without being rigid about it. It's equally important to help your child learn to adhere to routines and deal with change when necessary.

Bedtime can be difficult at this age, with resistance, repeated curtain calls, and occasional tantrums. Respond to requests in a matter-of-fact way, then leave the room. Or, if your toddler seems fearful and becomes unusually upset when you leave, sit quietly with her for a while, then try the "vanishing-chair routine." On successive nights, gradually move your chair closer toward the doorway, until it's finally outside the room (also see p. 139).

Nightmares tend to begin during the toddler years and are especially common during periods of stress, such as toilet training or the arrival of a new baby (see p. 134). Comfort your toddler and return him to his bed when calm but still awake. During the daytime, try to minimize the sources of stress.

Excessive daytime sleepiness, with yawning and napping at inappropriate times, is a sure sign that your school-age child is not getting enough sleep at night. But behavioral symptoms such as irritability, difficulty in concentrating, and forgetfulness may also signal that your youngster has a sleep problem. Some sleep-deprived children are mistakenly classed as hyperactive. In fact, their nonstop activity is a way of fighting off the daytime drowsiness that threatens to overwhelm them. Nightmares, sleep terrors, and sleep walking are also more frequent among youngsters with sleep troubles. (For hints in dealing with these and other sleep disturbances, see Chapter 8.)

PHYSICAL PROBLEMS THAT CAN INTERFERE WITH SLEEP

Sleep troubles are not diseases in themselves but, rather, symptoms that can signal the presence of physical or emotional problems. Such problems may be transient or chronic. Almost always, treatment of the underlying condition brings about a marked improvement in the quality and quantity of sleep.

EPILEPSY. Occasionally, symptoms of absence seizures (petit mal epilepsy) may be mistaken for daytime drowsiness or narcolepsy

Toddler Wakes Every Night

 Why does my 16-month-old wake at the same time every night?

Your toddler seems to be waking out of habit. Perhaps she was used to feeding at the same time every night. Or is she disturbed by a sound or light cue that occurs regularly?

If the cause is unwanted sound or light, make any necessary environmental changes. These could include leaving on a cool-mist humidifier or a radio tuned to static at low volume to make white noise, modifying the activities of family members (for example, keeping the TV quieter or running the bath at a different time), or installing shades to block out light. If no external trigger factor can be found, a behavioral approach may be needed.

Some sleep experts recommend scheduled awakenings to break the habit. To use this method, for several nights in a row, try awakening your child 10 or 15 minutes earlier than the time she usually wakes up, comfort her, and put her back to bed. On subsequent nights, wake her up progressively earlier until the habit of awakening is extinguished. Be sure to keep moving the waking time earlier in order to avoid simply resetting your child's clock so that she continues to awaken, but at a different time.

(see p. 188). A youngster with petit mal has recurrent "spells" during which she suddenly stops moving, her facial expression becomes blank, and her eyelids may flicker. The child does not fall down, as frequently happens with narcolepsy, but her head may fall forward slightly. Spells rarely last longer than 10 seconds at a time, but may recur frequently throughout the day. Typical childhood absence epilepsy is somewhat more common in girls, seldom

Three-Year-Old Obstinacy

? *Our 3-year-old still wakes up once or twice most nights. It's almost always so her father or I (we take turns) can pull the covers back over her. We've tried to show her how to pull up her own covers, but she simply refuses to do it. If we don't go in, she yells louder and becomes more awake. She's a fairly well-behaved, obedient child in most other respects. What can we do to get some shut-eye?*

Perhaps you could buy an inexpensive sleeping bag or blanket-sleeper pajamas. Explain to your daughter that although you will always help her if she's sick or something is wrong at night, you can no longer get up just to pull her bedclothes over her. Let her sleep in the zipped-up sleeping bag or blanket sleeper until she learns to pull up her own covers.

Too Excited to Sleep

Nighttime fears, separation anxiety, and school worries are among the commonest causes of wakefulness in school-age children. However, excitement and happy anticipation—the "night before Christmas" effect—are also powerful inhibitors of sleep. Be prepared for broken nights and daytime crankiness in the buildup to special events, such as birthdays and vacations.

Sustained over-excitement makes children crotchety and parents short-tempered. It can rob the long-awaited treat of all its joy. Either prepare for special events in a low-key way well in advance, letting the news gradually sink in, or save the announcement until the last possible minute to minimize the buildup period. The former method is appropriate for a major, permanent life change such as the birth of a new member of the family. The latter works better for one-time events, such as a trip to the circus.

HUNGER WAKES A TODDLER

? *My son, at 20 months, is still waking up at 2- to 3-hour intervals every night. He usually asks for a drink of juice or something to eat. His daytime caregiver has trouble getting him to eat because he drinks a lot of juice and has no appetite for solid foods.*

Your son may well be waking up because he's hungry. Some toddlers drink so much that they have no appetite for nourishing foods. Juices mainly provide calories that your youngster should get in a more nourishing form from solid foods. His appetite may improve if you offer water instead of juice when he's thirsty. Offer juice only in a cup, at scheduled snacks or meals. When your son is thirsty, he'll find water more thirst-quenching than sugary juice. Give your child's caregiver clear instructions about the feeding schedule and between-meals drinks.

---

appears before age 5, and, with treatment, usually disappears during adolescence. When absence epilepsy occurs in adolescence (juvenile absence epilepsy), spells are less frequent. If you suspect that your child may be having absence seizures, call your pediatrician for an evaluation.

Seizures occasionally affect sleeping children in pre- or early adolescence. These "sylvian" seizures generally occur as the child is beginning to awaken. They do not have lasting effects if appropriately treated. Consult your pediatrician if your child has movements resembling seizures while asleep.

OBSTRUCTIVE SLEEP APNEA. In spite of the many ongoing advances in children's health care, obstructive sleep apnea (also see p. 43) may be more of a problem now than it was 40 or 50 years ago. At that time, children's tonsils and adenoids were often removed rou-

SNORING IN A FOUR-YEAR-OLD WITH LARGE TONSILS

? *My son, 4 years old, snores loudly and wakes up several times every night. His tonsils look very large and I wonder if this could be causing sleep apnea?*

Young children's tonsils are normally much larger in relation to their body size than adults' tonsils. However, enlarged tonsils and adenoid tissue may also indicate that the child is in need of medical attention. The swollen tissues can block the airway, making it difficult to breathe. Thus, your child may wake up many times a night as he repeatedly chokes and then struggles to take a breath.

Loud snoring is not normal in a healthy child. Although there may be no connection between your son's snoring, his wakefulness, and his tonsils, call your pediatrician to schedule an examination.

tinely just because they appeared large. Thus, one of the risk factors for obstructive apnea—namely, bulky tissue that could block the airway as the muscles relaxed during sleep—was eliminated. More recently, the rate of tonsillectomies dropped sharply after it was recognized that the tonsils and adenoid tissue, as part of the infection-fighting lymphatic system, had an important part to play in keeping children free of illness. It is now recognized, too, that children's tonsils are normally much larger in relation to their body size than adults' tonsils. During the preschool years, children's tonsils gradually become larger, in relation to their body size, than adults' tonsils. This tonsil growth usually peaks at about 5 or 6 years of age. Then the tonsil size gradually recedes until, by adolescence, the airspace is larger and the youngster can breathe more freely. Pediatricians today seldom advise tonsillectomy except when children develop rare complications of infectious diseases, such as an abscess around the tonsils, or sleep apnea.

Sleep apnea is often hard to diagnose. Episodes occur at night, when the child is normally out of the parents' sight. Loud snoring may be dismissed as an odd quirk, rather than a signal that the child is fighting for breath; thus, the difficulty in breathing goes undetected.

Parents may be aware that their child sleeps poorly, wakes up many times a night, and seems tired and irritable during the day, but it may take a long time before the problems fall into a pattern that prompts a consultation with the family's pediatrician. Many children with large tonsils and adenoids never develop sleep apnea. Some are able to avert nighttime choking by switching from nose to mouth breathing as they sleep. And others have large enough airways, in spite of their large tonsils, that there's no problem.

If you have concerns about your child's snoring or noisy breathing, talk to your pediatrician. In many cases, noisy breathing is merely a symptom of a mild respiratory infection or allergy and will disappear as the underlying condition clears

NIGHT WAKING WITH COUGH

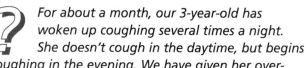 *For about a month, our 3-year-old has woken up coughing several times a night. She doesn't cough in the daytime, but begins coughing in the evening. We have given her over-the-counter medications without success.*

Call your pediatrician, who will examine your child and evaluate her respiratory system. Coughing that is worse at night or as a result of exposure to cold air can be a symptom of asthma, postnasal drip, or emotional upset, among other conditions. Over-the-counter medications should be used only on the advice of your pediatrician. If asthma is diagnosed, your pediatrician will prescribe treatment and help you identify asthma triggers and find ways to avoid exposing your child to them.

> Obstructive sleep apnea in older children should not be confused with the periodic breathing seen in infants (see Chapter 3). Periodic breathing in infants is not caused by airway obstruction. Instead, the baby just momentarily "forgets" to breathe. Most such episodes are of no concern. However, if your infant fails to take a breath for longer than 10 seconds, or has shorter periods of not breathing and symptoms such as fever or a change in skin color, **call the Emergency Medical Service**.

up. However, chronic apnea robs the child of sleep and leads to daytime sleepiness that interferes with the youngster's school performance and prevents him from functioning at the level of which he is capable. Several medical treatments are available for sleep apnea and, in some cases, surgery may be appropriate.

ALLERGIES AND ATOPIC DERMATITIS. Children with allergies often suffer broken nights because of stuffy noses, coughing, and other symptoms of allergy. Poor sleep is a particular problem for children with atopic dermatitis, a chronic, recurrent skin condition of which the hallmark symptom is itchy skin.

If allergy symptoms are keeping your child awake, your pediatrician may prescribe a short course of antihistamine medication. Drowsiness is a side effect of certain antihistamines; thus, by giving the dose at night, you may be able to help your child sleep better, in addition to relieving the allergy symptoms. If your child needs treatment in the daytime, your pediatrician may recommend a medication that does not cause drowsiness, to avoid problems at school.

Studies have shown that although children with atopic dermatitis usually blame itchiness for keeping them awake, these youngsters tend to have problems sleeping even during periods when they are symptom free. Many children with atopic dermatitis go on to develop asthma. In such cases, early, as-yet-unrecognized asthma symptoms may be among the causes of the sleep troubles. Researchers are investigating whether some of the sleep problems are the result of learned behavior, and what treatments can be used to ensure sound sleep with the least risk of side effects.

ASTHMA. Asthma is brought on by spasms in the tiny muscles of the airways and inflammation in the lining of the airways of the lungs. The spasms make the airways narrower, which makes it difficult for the child to breathe and causes a whistling or wheezing sound. A frequent symptom of asthma is a cough that gets worse at night, after exercise, or following contact with an irritant such as cigarette smoke or an allergen such as animal dander. Because the symptoms are more severe at night, children with asthma wake frequently and sleep poorly.

HEADACHES AND MIGRAINE. Children who have frequent headaches and migraine episodes have a high rate of sleep disturbances, including nighttime waking, daytime sleepiness, and poor sleep quality. Most adults are familiar with migraine as a condition marked by severe, throbbing, one-sided headaches and other symptoms. However, in children, migraine may also take the form of recurrent attacks of abdominal pain accompanied by nausea and vomiting, or episodes of irritability, hyperactivity,

HEADACHES MAY REQUIRE MEDICAL ATTENTION

If your child has frequent headaches, wakes up with a headache, has a sudden, severe headache, or has vomiting along with headache, bring it promptly to your pediatrician's attention. Most recurrent headaches are benign; however, your pediatrician may want to rule out a serious underlying condition.

confusion, and other symptoms with or without headache and vomiting. Youngsters with migraine tend to have more partial arousal disorders, such as sleepwalking and night terrors. In many cases, one or both parents have a history of headaches, migraine symptoms, and sleep troubles. Researchers theorize that the mechanisms behind migraine and partial arousals may originate in the same part of the brain.

A child with frequent headaches should be examined to make sure that there is no underlying problem. Only in rare cases is there a serious cause for headache. However, the majority of children actually suffer fewer headaches and less anxiety on receiving assurances from their pediatricians that nothing is wrong. Your pediatrician can recommend ways to identify and avoid trigger factors for your child's headache or migraine, and will advise about the use of pain relievers.

OVERWEIGHT. Early researchers who related daytime drowsiness in overweight children and adolescents to nighttime apnea (also see p. 60), or choking, believed that the apnea was caused mainly by pressure from excess fat deposits in the neck. However, recent studies indicated that the daytime sleepiness may also be related to metabolic, or energy-processing, abnormalities as well as disturbances in the circadian rhythms that can be brought on by extreme overweight.

The numbers of children and young people overweight enough to be termed "obese"—that is, 20 percent or more above their ideal weight for height—are rapidly rising. In the United States, at least one child in five is overweight. Over the last 20 years, the number of overweight children has increased by half, and the number of youngsters who should be considered extremely overweight has almost doubled.

Daytime sleepiness is only one of many health problems associated with the increase in body fat. Diabetes, heart trouble, and circulatory disorders are also severe, chronic conditions linked to overweight. Daytime somnolence leads, in turn, to difficulties with school performance, and children with sleep disorders tend to have more problems with behavior and paying attention.

If your child is overweight, ask your pediatrician for guidance with a nutritional plan designed to stabilize the weight. In case of severe overweight, your pediatrician may recommend consultation with a registered dietitian with experience in helping youngsters. Limit your child's TV watching and video and computer games to less than 2 hours a day. Get him moving in a program

Pinworms are found everywhere, in every age group and at all economic levels. They are especially common in children, and are easily passed from one child to another in group childcare and schools. Pinworms are annoying but generally harmless, although worms can carry bacteria from the anus to the female genital tract and cause infection.

Children swallow pinworm eggs carried under the fingernails, on clothing or bedding, or in house dust. The eggs hatch in the stomach and the larvae migrate to the intestine, where they mature into white worms about 1 centimeter (about ³/₈ inch) long. Female worms emerge at night to lay eggs near the child's anus. The child scratches the itching caused by the worms' movements and traps more eggs under the fingernails—only to swallow them again or shed them where they can find their way to new hosts.

If your child is having trouble getting to sleep, complains of itching, or is unusually fidgety, talk to your pediatrician. She may advise you to press clear, sticky cellophane tape around your child's anus in the morning. Eggs and worms adhering to the tape can help your pediatrician confirm the diagnosis.

Pinworms can be eradicated with a short course of medication. The treatment may need to be repeated from time to time, because reinfestation is common. Wash bedding and clothing in hot, soapy water to get rid of eggs and stop pinworms from spreading.

of regular, moderate exercise with the dual aims of replacing fat with muscle tissue and stimulating production of endorphins, the body's natural sleep inducers. Start with a modest goal—perhaps walking or swimming for half an hour every other day—and avoid exercise plans that are too taxing for your child's abilities. Join him in the activity if he doesn't like to exercise alone. Even more important than fixing the current weight problem is adopting a healthy, lifelong approach to eating, exercise, and sleep, which should help your youngster slim down.

RESTLESS LEGS. Many people often have trouble sleeping because of an uncomfortable, crawling feeling in their legs that goes away when they kick, flex their muscles, or get up and move about. To keep the description simple, doctors call this problem "restless legs syndrome" or RLS. The syndrome tends to become more common as people age, but it also occurs in children; one child referred to the feeling as "itchy bones." The cause is unknown, but the condition is seen slightly more often in those with iron-deficiency anemia, a relatively common nutritional deficiency. Many patients on kidney dialysis also have RLS.

If your child is having trouble sleeping because of RLS, your pediatrician may advise exercise and dietary measures, and possibly prescribe medication.

GASTROESOPHAGEAL REFLUX. Children occasionally wake up with a burning sensation in the chest and an acid taste in the mouth caused by gastroesophageal reflux, or GER. A ring of muscle at the bottom of the esophagus, the lower esophageal sphincter, normally relaxes to let food pass into the stomach, then tightens again to keep the food there. When the ring opens at the wrong time due to pressure or poorly timed relaxation, the stomach contents mixed with digestive acids flood back into the esophagus and cause the discomfort commonly called heartburn. In babies, GER is common, often associated with spitting up, and is rarely a concern; the baby grows out of it as his muscles mature. In older children, GER may occur after a large meal or one with a high fat content. Peppermint, caffeine, and certain medications including some used for asthma can cause the lower esophageal sphincter to relax at the wrong time. Some doctors believe that tomato-based foods have a similar effect.

If you can identify the food that causes GER in your child, keep it out of her diet for a week or two, then reintroduce it. If symptoms recur, it's probably best to avoid that food in future. A child with persistent GER needs medical attention. Your pediatrician may prescribe treatment to lessen the secretion of stomach acid or to help the lower esophageal sphincter muscle contract.

Sometimes, doctors advise that youngsters sit upright, instead of lounging on soft furniture or the floor, for an hour or two after dinner and before bed. It can also be helpful to raise the upper part of the child's body in bed with a wedge (available in pharmacies) to let gravity help the digestive tract work properly.

GROWING PAINS. Many girls and boys complain of muscle aches around bedtime, or wake up with pains in the legs and arms after sleeping for an hour or two. For want of a better explanation, these aches are called "growing pains." Although no one knows for sure what's behind them, growth is not the cause; even at the peak of the adolescent growth spurt, a youngster's rate of growth is too gradual to be painful.

Like many muscle aches in adults, growing pains are probably tenderness caused by overwork during hard exercise. Children don't feel sore while they're having fun; only later, when the muscles relax, do the pains come on.

You may not be able to prevent growing pains, but you can help your child lessen the aches. Call for periodic rest breaks during energetic play and encourage your youngster to take part in a variety of sports and activities. In this way, he'll give different muscle groups a workout and avoid overstraining the same muscles day after day. A warm bath before bedtime may help soothe muscles and ease aches. When growing pains are bothersome,

TIME TO GET HELP FOR MUSCLE PAINS

Call your pediatrician if your child has any of the following symptoms:

■ Severe pain.

■ Swelling that doesn't decrease or that grows worse after 24 hours, despite first aid with RICE (rest, ice or a cool compress, compression, and elevation) treatment.

■ Fever.

■ A persistent lump in a muscle.

gently massage your child's limbs; a dose of children's acetaminophen or ibuprofen may be helpful.

STOMACHACHE. Youngsters complain of stomachaches for all sorts of reasons—not least, to stall at bedtime. Or perhaps they're trying to avoid school. A viral infection such as influenza may be causing the pain. Or maybe somebody has just eaten "not wisely but too well." Recurrent abdominal pain is common but, luckily, not often serious in children. In many cases, no physical cause can be found, and the pain is termed "functional" or nonspecific pain, possibly related to emotional stress. At times, spasms in the digestive tract may cause pain. A crying child may swallow gas, which can cause abdominal discomfort. What's essential to remember is that the pain can be real, even though there is no obvious cause.

Abdominal pain that either comes on suddenly or persists may require prompt attention, especially if your child has additional symptoms, such as a change in the bowel pattern, vomiting, fever (temperature higher than 101°F or 38.3°C), swelling, sore throat, or headache. Even when no physical cause can be found, the child's distress is genuine and should receive appropriate attention. Call your pediatrician promptly if your baby under age 1 shows signs of stomach pain (legs pulled up toward the abdomen, unusual crying), your child age 4 or younger has recurrent stomachache, or if abdominal pain wakes your child or stops him from getting to sleep.

ABDOMINAL PAIN MAY BE A SYMPTOM OF LEAD POISONING

Vague abdominal pain is one of several symptoms that may be associated with lead poisoning in children. If you live in an older home that has peeling paint or is being renovated, and if your child often has stomachaches, appears unusually pale and tired, has frequent headaches, or has learning and behavior problems and seems to be less advanced than other youngsters the same age, raise this concern with your pediatrician, who will examine your child and order any necessary diagnostic tests.

Medications May Cause Sleeplessness

Several medications widely used to treat children's ailments can interfere with sleep. For example, doctors treating children with asthma generally try to match the child with a medication that carries the lowest risk of side effects; however, several anti-asthma medications are based on compounds that can keep children awake. If your child is under treatment for asthma and is having difficulty falling asleep or staying asleep, ask your pediatrician whether the dosage needs to be adjusted or the medication changed.

Similarly, numerous cold, allergy, and sinus remedies sold without prescription can make the user feel jittery and wakeful. These and any nonprescription medications should not be given to children except on the advice of your pediatrician.

While medications prescribed for children with attention deficit/hyperactivity disorder (ADHD) are intended to improve concentration and help the child control his behavior, side effects can sometimes include sleeplessness. Some sedatives and medications given to control seizures can make children sleepy in the daytime and thus interfere with the normal nighttime sleep. Your pediatrician may be able to revise the dosage schedule to enable your child to rest at the proper time.

When no other cause can be found for a school-age child's wakefulness, caffeine often proves to be the culprit. Most people are aware that regular coffee and tea can interfere with sleep, but fewer understand that the decaffeinated versions also contain some caffeine. Children are not generally heavy consumers of hot coffee and tea, but many drink iced tea, especially the sweetened, fruit-flavored iced teas sold as year-round soft drinks. Colas and many other soft drinks also deliver caffeine in doses that can interfere with children's sleep.

There's no harm in letting your child have a soft drink as an occasional treat, but soda pop should not be part of a regular diet for at least three reasons. First, not only does the caffeine content make children wakeful but, second, these drinks also contain large amounts of sugar. Studies have failed to prove a link between sugar consumption and hyperactivity or sleeplessness.

Melatonin, a hormone secreted by the brain's pineal gland, allows the body to tell the difference between light and darkness. In humans, who normally sleep at night and remain awake during the day, melatonin release is a signal to shut down for sleep. By contrast, in nocturnal animals, melatonin release is the cue to get ready for the night's activities.

The hormone helps to regulate hibernation, sexual activity, and the production of sex hormones in mammals other than humans. Its effects in humans are not fully understood, but it is known that a permanent drop in the melatonin level is a necessary step before puberty can begin. Though not approved as a safe and effective drug in humans, melatonin is widely sold under the label of a dietary supplement. Until more is known about the link between melatonin levels and sexual maturation, *melatonin should not be given to children and adolescents*. It is possible, for example, that by giving melatonin to a youngster and thus keeping circulating levels of the hormone artificially high, you could delay puberty and interfere with normal development.

Occasionally, doctors may recommend melatonin treatment for developmentally disabled or blind children. Such children can have severe sleep problems due to their inability to establish normal circadian rhythms based on the light/dark cycle. Melatonin treatment should never be attempted except as prescribed and supervised by your child's doctor.

On the contrary, in several studies, children given high doses of sugar tended to become drowsy sooner than those who did not get sugar. However, sugar promotes the action of bacteria that cause tooth decay. Frequent sipping on sweetened drinks over the course of the day immerses the teeth in a sugar bath that can hasten the development of cavities. Finally, soft drinks deliver lots of

FOODS FOR SLEEP

 I have heard that children's nutrition can play a role in sleeping habits. What should I look for in the foods my youngsters eat?

Foods affect sleep in several ways. Certain foods induce drowsiness; others tend to keep people awake; and sensitivity or allergy to foods can bring on symptoms that interfere with sleep. A young child may wake up crying if he feels hungry, or may have trouble falling asleep if his stomach is overfull.

Foods that promote sleep include complex carbohydrates, such as in cereals, whole-grain breads and pasta, and legumes (dried peas and beans); and B vitamins, found in the complex carbohydrates as well as nuts and seeds, poultry, meat, seafood, and dairy foods. Another sleep inducer is calcium, plentiful in many different foods, especially milk and milk products. A high calcium content is also found in broccoli, tofu, and any canned fish that is eaten bones and all (canned salmon, sardines). The amino acid L-tryptophan (an essential nutrient found in meat, poultry, milk, eggs, whole-grain breads and

calories from sugar, but next to nothing in the way of valuable nutrients. Thus, they may contribute to excess weight gain and take the place of more healthful foods.

SLEEP AND FOOD ALLERGY OR INTOLERANCE

True food allergies are uncommon, affecting no more than about 2 out of 100 people. Still, children may have sleep problems because of symptoms related to food allergy or—more commonly—food intolerance. In true food allergy, the immune system tries to fight proteins in the offending food as if they were cereals, pasta, soy, peanuts, and a variety of other foods) also promotes sleep.

Caffeine, present in coffee, tea, colas, and many other soft drinks, stimulates the nervous system and promotes wakefulness. Foods with a high fat content take longer to pass out of the stomach and can cause the acidic stomach contents to flow back into the esophagus, leading to discomfort and wakefulness due to indigestion. Alcohol makes people sleepy at first but causes wakefulness later during the night; of course, alcohol has no place in children's and adolescents' diets.

Food allergies are not common and thus seldom cause sleep problems. However, foods that may cause symptoms of allergy or sensitivity, possibly including sleep problems, are cow's milk and products made from cow's milk, egg white, wheat, soy, peanuts, tree nuts (such as walnuts and pecans), shellfish, and chocolate. Some people are also allergic to corn. If you suspect that your child has symptoms, including sleep problems, related to allergies or food intolerance, ask your pediatrician for an evaluation.

alien invaders like bacteria or viruses. Food intolerance, by contrast, is an inability to digest a particular food, usually because the person lacks an enzyme necessary for the process. Typical symptoms of allergy and intolerance include runny nose, nausea and/or vomiting, loose stools, wheezing, skin rash, and itching, all of which can keep a child awake.

Although allergies and intolerances cannot be cured, the severity of symptoms can be controlled by avoiding the offending foods or—as in the well-known case of lactose intolerance—substituting a food that has been processed to make it more digestible, such as lactose-free milk. Food allergy can also involve cross-reactions with non-food substances. Fortunately, almost half of children who develop food allergies before age 3 grow out of the problem by about age 7, and 95 percent of babies who have the common allergy to cow's milk outgrow it by age 3. Children who develop allergies after age 3 are less likely to grow out of them.

If food allergy or intolerance is diagnosed in your child, learn to recognize alternative names for the offending food (calcium caseinate for cow's milk protein is one example) and familiarize yourself with the range of foods that may contain the allergen in hidden form (such as high-fructose corn syrup in soft drinks, or peanuts in some chocolate chips). Always read food labels carefully and teach your child to do the same when he is old enough.

CHAPTER 5

Controversies and Strategies

Most babies sleep for 2 to 3 hours at a time for the first two weeks or so, soon extending sleep periods to 4- to 5-hour stretches, with correspondingly fewer breast- or bottle-feeding breaks and longer periods of alertness and play. However, well-meaning grandparents and friends may ask, "Is the baby sleeping through the night?" so often that a continuous stretch of nighttime sleep takes on an unrealistic importance. If the magic milestone hasn't appeared by 6 or 8 weeks, the parents wonder if there's something wrong with their child or the way they are looking after him.

Sleep is only a step behind feeding among the aspects of baby care most likely to make new parents anxious. Parents are concerned not only about their baby's sleep, but also their own. After all, if the baby can't sleep, neither can they.

In fact, completely unbroken nights may still be far in the future. About 90 percent of all babies regularly sleep through the night by age 3 months, but for some it takes longer. Sleeping through the night actually means 5 to 6 hours of sleep without waking. So if your baby goes down for the night at about 8:00 o'clock, you may expect to be up for the next change and feeding between 1:00 and 3:00 in the morning. Of course, you can adjust this time span by feeding your baby and putting him to bed later. But even after your child has achieved the breakthrough of sleeping through the night, the sleep pattern will change again.

In the early years, most children vary their nighttime routine from time to time. They may sleep undisturbed for weeks or months, then abruptly go back to late-night waking for a while. There are many reasons for waking. Perhaps your baby needs more food to fuel a growth spurt, in which case your pediatrician may advise introducing solid foods. Teething may be making the baby's mouth sore. Or the baby may have taken a leap in development that involves a temporary change in the sleeping pattern.

Even at this early age, your baby is an individual with certain likes and dislikes (see *Sleep and Temperament*, p. 111) and it's unreasonable to try and control every detail of her behavior. You can't force your child to sleep; what you can do is help her learn that nighttime is for sleeping and daytime for play, and to develop regular sleep habits. Most important, you can help her learn to

When Your Baby Cries at Night

During the first several months, the best way to manage crying is to respond promptly whenever your infant cries. It's impossible to spoil a young baby by giving her attention; if you answer her cries for help, she'll cry less overall.

When attending to your crying baby, try to address her most urgent problem first. For example, if she's cold and hungry and has a wet diaper, wrap her to warm her up, change her diaper, then feed her. If her crying has a desperate quality, suggesting she's in pain, quickly check for an open diaper pin or a strand of hair wound around a finger or toe. When your baby is calm again but still awake, put her back in her crib, say your good nights, and leave the room. If she cries again after you leave, give her a few minutes to settle on her own. Many babies go to sleep more quickly if left for a while. If the crying keeps up, repeat your visits at increasingly longer intervals, but no longer than 10 minutes at a time. Keep the room dim, speak quietly and no more than you have to, and avoid picking your baby up.

comfort herself and go back to sleep the several times a night when, like all babies, she partly awakens but doesn't need to be fed or changed.

Babies and children thrive on a regular routine. This doesn't mean that you have to keep to a rigid schedule. Rather, the more your child can look forward to events rolling out in a predictable sequence, the easier it is to cope with occasional exceptions to the rule, such as when bedtime or a meal is unavoidably delayed. It's never too early to teach a child to sleep well or too late to change a bad habit. Children are adaptable and eager to learn. It's up to parents to take the initiative for change and stick to it, even though the adjustment period may be difficult.

TOYS IN CRIBS

It is unsafe to place pillows, bulky covers, and large stuffed toys in your young infant's crib. However, there's no harm in tucking a small, soft toy in a corner. Your baby will look forward to seeing its familiar features last thing before he goes to sleep and first thing on waking. By about 6 months, he'll start to play with it. And in time, he may choose it for a "cuddly" or "lovey"—a transitional object that helps him feel safe, calm, and relaxed for sleep.

SLEEPING THROUGH THE NIGHT

If your child is not sleeping 5 to 6 hours through the night by 3 months, you may help the process along by keeping him awake longer in the afternoon and early evening. Make sure he has plenty of stimulation during his waking periods: toys, perhaps a "busy box," a brightly patterned rug to lie on, music to listen to, and most of all, someone to talk with. This may help stop him from being lulled into sleep earlier than necessary. On the other hand, don't keep a sleepy baby up for the sake of pushing his bedtime back by a few minutes. A child who is overtired will become upset and find it hard to settle down.

Preventing Bedtime Resistance

Even a baby a few weeks old may have trouble winding down after a day crowded with activities and people. Keep bedtime calm, with a regular routine, and avoid stimulating play in the evening. Give your attention to your baby during the bedtime routine, and concentrate on low-key activities, such as repetitive songs or nursery rhymes and picture books. When the routine is done, place him still awake in his bed. It's not a good idea to prop your baby on your lap and expect him to become drowsy while you watch a video or TV program. The bright, rapidly shifting images and jarring sounds may overstimulate the baby's still-developing nervous system and keep him wide awake.

Maintaining a Twenty-Four-Hour Cycle

The natural biological, or circadian, rhythms—including the sleep/wake cycle—follow a 24-hour cycle, but, left unregulated, the timing of the rhythms may shift later. The circadian rhythms are best maintained by a consistent routine with regular cues for activities and functions. Waking at about the same time every morning is one of the most important cues for keeping circadian rhythms keyed to a 24-hour day.

From the beginning, it's wise to put your baby in the crib while he is drowsy but still awake. This helps him link being in the crib with the pleasant feeling of falling asleep. (Psychologists call this forming a "positive sleep association.") It also helps to orient the baby when he wakes up, so that as time goes on, he will lie quietly for a while or explore his crib toys, enjoying a little time on his own before calling for attention.

When you have completed the going-to-bed ritual, place your baby in her crib, still awake. Say your good nights, turn on the night-light (a low-wattage table lamp may be better than a plug-in night-light if it causes scary shadows), and leave the room.

Whether or not you close the door is up to you. Many children become distressed when they hear that final "click" that cuts them off from the rest of the household. Shutting the door also makes it harder for you to hear your child if she cries or silently to check on her. Leaving the door partly open and a dim hall light on can often forestall problems. (However, before you go to bed, shut the doors to all sleeping rooms. The American Academy of Pediatrics recommends that doors to sleeping rooms be kept shut at night as a fire safety measure.)

Nighttime Waking After Four or Five Months

Opinions differ widely about the "right" way to manage night time wakings from about the middle of the first year. At one end of the scale is the childcare authority who insists that from the moment of settling the baby and leaving the bedroom, parents shouldn't go back except to rescue the child in a life-threatening emergency. The baby, he says, should be left to cry it out, no matter how long "it" may take, and parents should sit out the siege as far as possible from the baby's room, shutting all doors in between to muffle the sound of crying. He advises against changing diapers during the night; instead, parents are told to apply liberal quantities of zinc oxide ointment to their baby's bottom before bed to prevent rashes caused by prolonged exposure to wet or soiled diapers. To reassure parents who are apprehensive about leaving their baby to cry for 3 to 4 hours at a stretch, he says, "crying produces accelerated forgetting of a learned response— we are leaving him alone to forget the expectation to be picked up." In other words, the more you leave your infant to cry, the sooner he'll forget that you used to pick him up when he cried. This approach, though, is unduly harsh.

At the other extreme is the school of thought whose adherents insist that babies should always fall asleep at the breast or with a bottle, preferably in the parents' bed. The baby, they say, should be offered a feeding whenever he stirs during the night. This approach, too, has major drawbacks for many parents. Although some families prefer togetherness in a family bed, many others

Crying is the only way a young baby can make his needs and wants known. When your baby cries, he's trying to tell you something or to wind down after a stimulating day; he's not doing it to annoy you. Pediatricians advise that babies tend to cry less overall if their calls for help are answered promptly. Thus, for parents, the important thing is to be able to tell one kind of cry from another, and most parents learn this in the first few weeks of their baby's life.

find that constant co-sleeping means less—and less restful—sleep. Scientific studies back them up: Children and adults alike sleep longer and better in individual beds. The American Academy of Pediatrics cautions against co-sleeping in a family bed because of the increased risk of sudden infant death. (Read about the risks that may be associated with co-sleeping in *Sharing a Bed with Your Baby*, p. 90.)

A further disadvantage of co-sleeping is that breastfed babies who are allowed to nurse at will during the night continue to awaken for night feedings long after the need has passed. The breast is assigned the role of a pacifier; without it, the baby has difficulty settling down to sleep. These babies feed out of habit, not because they need the nourishment. The unlimited night feedings can also be a source of excess calories that open the door to lifelong struggles with overweight. Finally, when the time inevitably comes to stop nighttime feedings and reclaim the bed, some parents find that they have only postponed, not avoided, bedtime resistance and night waking.

To ensure peaceful nights for everyone, it's probably easier to follow a middle path. It isn't necessary to rush into your child's room the moment you hear a whimper, but neither do you and your baby have to suffer increasingly distressed sobs for hours on end. Young children normally cry out or babble during periods of semi-arousal several times every night. In almost all cases, they go back to sleep on their own. As you get to know your baby, you soon learn to distinguish the fussing sounds as he settles down, his hunger cry, the sad cries that tell you he is distressed, and an angry bellow for attention.

If your child needs a clean diaper or other care, provide what he needs with the minimum of disturbance: Keep the lights dim; speak softly and no more than you need to; change the diaper and put the baby right back to bed or change him in the crib if you can; and quickly leave the room, as at bedtime. If your baby's crying persists longer than, say, 5 minutes after you leave (5 minutes is an arbitrary number; the real one is how many minutes you can stand to hear your baby cry, and 5 to 10 minutes is a general guideline), go back into the room without turning on the light,

Crying Helps Babies Unwind

Many babies cry quite hard right after their parents leave the bedroom. In most cases, the crying stops abruptly after a few minutes and the baby settles down to sleep. This is the way the baby winds down emotionally after a day crammed with stimulation. Don't rush back to your baby at the first cry. He probably doesn't need attention. On the contrary, he probably wants a little time on his own to sort out a jumble of feelings and impressions.

pat your baby or gently rub him and quietly tell him it's time to sleep, then leave again. Repeat your visits at progressively longer intervals within the 5- to 10-minute range and be firm: no picking up. If you pick him up, you'll only disappoint him with false hopes. Expecting a lengthy cuddle, your baby will redouble his crying when you put him down again, and sleepiness will be delayed even further.

Monitor the crying for any change and manage the inevitable false alarms in the same low-key way. It's better to respond promptly to a cry that sounds like a distress call than to ignore it and lie awake wondering if your baby is *really* all right.

Common Causes of Sleep Problems in Infants

PAIN AND ILLNESS. A vast range of factors can interfere with sleep starting in the earliest months of life. A baby may wake because of fever and pain due to an ear infection or an upset stomach,

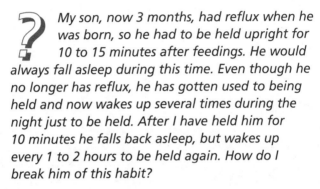

LEARNING NEW SLEEP ASSOCIATIONS

My son, now 3 months, had reflux when he was born, so he had to be held upright for 10 to 15 minutes after feedings. He would always fall asleep during this time. Even though he no longer has reflux, he has gotten used to being held and now wakes up several times during the night just to be held. After I have held him for 10 minutes he falls back asleep, but wakes up every 1 to 2 hours to be held again. How do I break him of this habit?

While you held your baby to prevent his stomach contents from flowing back into his esophagus, he enjoyed the sensation of being cuddled or rocked to sleep. Now your challenge is to help him learn new positive sleep associations (see p. 78). Cuddle and quietly play with your baby during your bedtime routine, then put him in his crib sleepy but still awake. Place a small, soft toy in his crib where he can see it as he falls asleep and wake up to it in the morning. Eventually he may adopt it as his "lovey" or transitional object—a further aid to relaxation and sleep. Leave the room and return at increasingly longer intervals to pat your baby gently and reassure him with your voice, but don't pick him up. Manage further wakings during the night in a similar way: Go to your baby's room, leave the lights off (except a night-light), pat your baby and speak softly to him, but don't pick him up. Leave the room when he is drowsy but still awake.

such as with mild gastroenteritis. A hair or thread caught around your baby's finger may be painful; sometimes a little boy can be in pain from a hair wound around his penis. Or an arm or leg caught in the crib bars may need to be untangled.

Discomfort from teething may begin as early as 3 months. If a baby is sleeping poorly, vomiting or spitting up large amounts of milk, and seems to have abdominal pain, your pediatrician may want to investigate the cause. Symptoms may be due to a milk allergy or to irritation caused when acidic stomach contents flow back into the esophagus (gastroesophageal reflux). Even a minor illness can have a lasting effect on sleep because, while it lasts, the parents are especially responsive to the baby's distress. The baby, in turn, enjoys the extra attention and continues to cry for it after the symptoms have cleared up.

The results of several studies have shown that babies born after a long or difficult labor tend to wake more at night during their first year than infants with uncomplicated births. However, when the researchers looked at the reasons, the babies from difficult deliveries were just as healthy as the others; they woke up only because their parents worried more about them and consequently picked them up more often.

TEMPERAMENT. In time, most babies naturally fall into regular sleep patterns, thanks to an inborn temperament that allows them a good level of adaptability (also see *Sleep and Temperament*, p. 111). Those who are more difficult to settle may have less well-established biological rhythms, may be more sensitive to stimuli, and may be intense, excitable personalities who cry harder and louder than other babies, thus forcing themselves awake and finding it harder to calm down. Even at an early age, some babies show a low level of adaptability, which makes it difficult for them to accept change. A wide temperamental gap between baby and parents—say, an excitable child with a short attention span and a rigidly methodical father, or a shy, withdrawn child and a loud, extroverted mother—adds to the difficulty of setting routines. Extra patience, more time, and a change in parenting style may be needed to establish regular sleep habits in these highly sensitive infants. Your pediatrician can advise you and may refer you to a

Parents May Be Overinvolved

> Sleep problems may start because parents provide unnecessary nighttime feeding, soothing, or other stimulation. As long as they continue, their children will also persist in demanding nonstop entertainment. When parents recognize their contribution to the problem and withdraw the attention, most children accept the change after a short transition period. Children are fast learners who quickly adapt to changes in the routine. They also deserve time on their own without parental intervention, to learn how to soothe and occupy themselves.

counselor or a support group for parents with similar challenges.

SEPARATION ANXIETY. Beginning in the second half of the first year, separation anxiety causes many broken nights (also see p. 19). While it lasts, a baby or toddler may wake several times and cry anxiously for one or both parents, often expressing a strong preference for one. A toddler may try to climb out of her crib, cling desperately, and plead to be allowed to sleep in her parents' bed. She isn't being naughty or manipulative. This is a normal stage in children's emotional development and needs to be managed with a loving and consistent approach. Separation anxiety usually fades away somewhere around the second birthday. Until it does so, your child may need reassurance several times night after night.

You can take steps during the day to lessen nighttime disturbances:

- No matter how young your baby is, let him know in a matter-of-fact way when you have to leave him. Even if you're only going into another room for a minute, tell him, "I'll be right back." One day he'll surprise you with his own, "Right back!" when he's leaving you for a while.
- Playing peek a boo and games in the mirror helps your baby to understand that Mommy and Daddy go away and come back.
- When you go out in the evening, try to use a familiar baby-

sitter. If you must use a new one, ask her to arrive before the child's bedtime and allow a little time for getting acquainted. Many parents make it a rule to employ a regular baby-sitter one night a week and plan their social activities accordingly. Children usually find it easy to accept such a separation when it is part of a predictable routine.

HOW SOME BAD HABITS FORM

A few common habits that parents fall into, though with the best of intentions, can disrupt the family's sleep in the first few years of life:

- Allowing your baby to fall asleep at the breast or bottle.
- Rocking your baby to sleep.
- Sharing a bed with your baby.

These practices are not always necessarily harmful in themselves, but two can involve serious risks to health. For example, allowing a baby to go to sleep with a bottle of breastmilk, formula, or juice can cause serious tooth decay, called "nursing bottle caries," which badly affects not only the baby teeth but the permanent teeth as well (also see p. 39). This practice can also increase the risk of ear infections, a frequent cause of broken nights and lost sleep. And small babies are in danger of being suffocated when sharing a bed with larger family members. Roll-over deaths may account for some of the deaths reported due to sudden infant death syndrome (SIDS) each year. Health risks aside, the main drawback of these habits, in the long term, is to hamper the development of self-reliance in the child. Most of all, they stop both child and parents from getting a good night's sleep.

FALLING ASLEEP AT THE BREAST OR BOTTLE. "My baby can't settle down to sleep unless she is nursing." "I have to give my child a bottle or he cries himself to sleep." These babies have been taught to associate feeding and sleeping in such a way that the breast or bottle and the mother are part of the going-to-sleep routine, and the baby cannot fall asleep without it. Some pediatricians describe the mothers of such babies as "too good," because they do so much more than the child wants or needs. By anticipating every

Of course you want to give your baby every comfort when she's falling asleep, and it's tempting to take advantage of the natural lull that comes over the baby as she reaches the end of a nursing period with her tummy full.

However, when a mother makes it a rule to encourage her child to fall asleep while nursing, she may be sending a controlling message that she doesn't intend, at least consciously. What she is telling the baby, in effect, is "You can't go to sleep without me," just when her baby is beginning the long struggle to develop a sense of individuality and independence.

whim, they prevent their children from developing a natural ability to soothe themselves.

For some infants and their mothers, a final breast- or bottle-feeding is a comforting, calming part of the preparing-for-bed routine. But the breast or bottle is not a pacifier. If your baby needs extra comfort from sucking to fall asleep, help her find her thumb or give her a pacifier. Many children suck their thumbs and fingers for comfort while falling asleep and at no other time. More than half of all thumb-suckers stop before the end of their first year. No matter what old wives' tales may say, thumb-sucking is a normal habit. Most children eventually wean themselves of the thumb-sucking habit without any intervention. In most cases it is unlikely to distort the tooth alignment. Children who are still sucking the thumb day and night by age 5, when the permanent teeth begin to emerge, are the exception.

Some parents continue to offer the breast or bottle whenever their babies cry at night, long after the babies have stopped requiring night feedings. Older breastfed infants tend to wake and cry more often at night than formula-fed infants. Although breastmilk passes out of a baby's stomach faster than formula does, pediatricians generally discount hunger as the cause of the crying. Rather, as with several other sleep problems that have

A THREE-YEAR-OLD WAKING TO NURSE

 My son just turned 3 years old and still is not sleeping through the night because he wakes up to breastfeed. How do I stop this?

The decision to stop breastfeeding is a highly personal one and varies considerably according to cultural customs and individual preferences. However, by age 3, your child no longer benefits from the maternal antibodies that protected him in infancy, and he should be getting all the nutrients he needs from a varied and balanced diet. By now he is waking up out of habit and not because he is hungry and needs to nurse.

You may either explain to your child that the time for nursing is over and no longer offer him the breast at night, or you may shorten the time for nursing by about 2 minutes for several nights in a row, until you have reached a duration of about 2 minutes, then stop offering the breast altogether. In either case, your child will probably continue to wake up at night, since this is his habit. If he cannot settle back to sleep without a drink, as he is used to, let him have a small drink of water in a cup. Do not offer a bottle or suggest milk or juice. Your son does not need these fluids for nutrition at night, and the sugars they contain can remain in his mouth as he sleeps and foster tooth decay. Help your youngster settle back in his own bed, and leave the room while he is drowsy but still awake. Both you and your son may need a little time to adjust to the new system. If you experience persistent difficulties, talk to your pediatrician or your own physician.

their start in parents' behavior, these babies and their mothers continue nursing at night from habit or a desire for company.

To break the habit, most pediatricians recommend phased withdrawal rather than the "cold turkey" method. When the child wakes during the night, the parents should briefly check to make sure there is no physical reason for the crying. If the child is older than about 6 months, the amount of breastmilk or formula given at night should be tapered off, the duration of the feeding shortened, and the feedings finally discontinued altogether. Many pediatricians advise diluting nighttime bottle-feedings with water. Start by replacing a quarter of the usual amount of milk or formula with water, and increase the dilution over several nights until the bottle contains nothing but water. At this point, babies generally lose interest and stop waking for the nighttime feeding. A bottle-fed baby may cry less if the withdrawal visits are managed by the parent who does not usually provide the nighttime feedings and thus is not associated with the routine.

In most cases, it should be possible to complete the withdrawal process within 2 weeks. Once the feedings are stopped, nighttime crying should be managed with a brief initial visit to make sure there isn't a physical problem. If the crying continues, return for brief visits at increasingly longer intervals—between 5 and 10 minutes at a time. Speak in a soft, reassuring tone to your baby, pat him or rub him gently, but *don't pick him up*. The sooner you make the change, the easier it will be. However, make sure you choose a time to change when your baby doesn't need extra attention because of an illness with uncomfortable symptoms. If you are concerned about letting your baby cry for a longer period than usual because it may wake your other children or disturb the neighbors, choose a weekend or school vacation time when the crying will be less disruptive. If you live in an apartment building, let your neighbors know what you're trying to do, in case the crying may upset them.

There are parents who simply cannot bear to hear their baby cry, even for a minute or two. In such cases, a workable solution may be to agree on a plan whereby the more sensitive parent uses earplugs, takes a walk, or otherwise keeps busy and leaves the other partner to deal with the bedtime routine.

ROCKING A FUSSY BABY TO SLEEP. Few sounds are more upsetting

A baby who continues to cry after being picked up may settle faster if you put her back in her crib. A tired infant is irritable, and crying with fatigue is a sign that she needs to be handled less, not more. When you pick up a tired, cranky baby or try to distract her, she becomes overstimulated and then finds it almost impossible to calm down.

or puzzling to parents than the fussy or colicky crying that comes on without warning in the first few weeks of their baby's life. Colic is marked by hours of inconsolable screaming that starts at about the same time every day, lasts for hours, and recurs for weeks on end. Bouts of colic usually begin when babies are between 2 and 4 weeks old, and frequently taper off between $2^1/2$ and 4 months, although some babies are still colicky at 6 months. About one baby in every five develops colic, and first-born babies and boys are more likely to be colicky than later-born children and girls.

Not all babies have colic, but most have at least a daily period of fussy crying that leaves the parents or caregivers feeling helpless and frustrated. While the crying is going on, nothing seems to help, and yet the crying usually stops as abruptly as it started, and the baby quickly falls asleep.

The causes of colic and fussy crying are unknown and there is no cure, but all babies eventually outgrow this phase. It may simply be a stage in the maturation of the nervous system, during which babies have difficulty processing the vast amount of sensory input they receive each day. Whatever the cause may be, parents find by trial and error that many colicky babies can be calmed, at least some of the time, by swaddling (wrapping the baby firmly in a receiving blanket), sucking (a breast, bottle, finger, or pacifier), and rhythmic movement (gentle rocking, walking, swinging). Music, white noise—a steady sound supplied by a recording or a radio tuned to static—and the rhythmical sounds of household appliances (see p. 50) have all been used successfully to quiet colicky infants. However, what works today may not work tomorrow, and many parents develop a whole repertory of calming strategies until, one day, the colic or fussy crying simply stops and never comes back.

Rocking is helpful as long as it is used to calm the baby before he is placed, still awake, in the crib. If babies are regularly rocked to sleep, they come to depend on rocking long after the reason for it—that is, fussy crying or colic—has come and gone. At first, you rock because the baby is fussy; later, the baby gets fussy unless you rock. As with needlessly offering the breast or bottle, picking up the baby and rocking her every time she whimpers stifles her ability to learn self-soothing skills. Also, keeping the baby aroused with unnecessary attention and movement robs both her and you of your much-needed rest.

It's understandable that many parents get into a habit of "preventive rocking": anything to stop the desperate cries of a fussy, colicky infant. But while it's only natural to try to comfort your baby, there's little you can do either to prevent or stop the crying bouts. This is a phase that the baby outgrows. Sleep experts agree that factors that disturb sleep in the first several weeks of life, such as colic, are inherent and self-limited, whereas after 4 months, poor sleep habits are learned and not inborn.

SHARING A BED WITH YOUR BABY. The American Academy of Pediatrics cautions against routine co-sleeping in a family bed. Tiny infants can be smothered under bedclothes or the weight of a much larger body. Co-sleeping—parents and children sharing a bed—is a widespread practice in many cultures and it is claimed that children suffer no long-lasting ill effects. However, what's often overlooked is that in countries where co-sleeping is routinely practiced, families almost never sleep in beds with soft mattresses and bulky covers. A baby may be less likely to smother when the family sleeps on a floor mat with only a light coverlet.

The U.S. Consumer Product Safety Commission (USCPSC) opposes bed sharing by infants and adults, particularly if there is more than one adult in the bed. Many cases of infant suffocation have been reported due to bed sharing. However, the USCPSC recognizes that many mothers co-sleep with their

Give Sleep a Chance

? *My daughter, who is 7 months, seems to have a problem with falling asleep by herself or staying in her crib at night. She doesn't have a problem with naps during the day. I have tried various ways except for "letting her cry"; I don't feel comfortable with that idea. She falls asleep in less than a minute when her head touches our mattress, so she sleeps in the family bed at night. Now, after 7 months of sharing, I'm not getting enough sleep, my back hurts, and my husband has moved to the couch.*

The answer is not to let her cry, but rather, to let her fall asleep. Your baby falls asleep without difficulty when you leave her in her crib for daytime naps. However, she can't do so at night because she is always moved to the family bed before she's asleep. Thus, she's learned that the family bed is where she sleeps at night and has become used to going to sleep on your mattress.

Help your baby learn some new sleep associations. Put her in her crib sleepy but still awake. Leave a night-light on or leave the door ajar so light shines in from the hallway; she may feel uneasy when her room is totally dark. After saying your good nights, leave the room and give your baby time to settle. If she continues to cry, return at increasingly longer intervals (between 5 and 10 minutes) to pat or rub her and quietly soothe her with your voice, but don't pick her up.

Be consistent, to make the learning process easier on your baby. If you pick her up, she will expect to be carried to the family bed. When her rhythm is disturbed in this way she is likely to become wide awake, and then have to start falling asleep all over again.

DEALING WITH A DIFFERENT POINT OF VIEW

? *Friends encourage my partner and me to allow our baby to sleep with us in a family bed. They warn us that our failure to "nighttime parent" will cause our child to be insecure and that our approach—having our child sleep in a crib and letting him cry for a while as long as he's not uncomfortable—is inhumane. This method has worked for us; our child sleeps well. Of course, if he awakens during the night and cries persistently, we go in at once to see if anything's wrong. However, I now feel guilty about doing something that others consider to be child abuse. Could a method that works so well be wrong in the long run because, as our friends claim, it promotes psychological damage?*

Time and again in this book, we emphasize that there are few cut-and-dried solutions to children's sleep problems. The best solution is the one that works for your family.

It sounds as if you have found such a solution: Your child sleeps well and receives as much nighttime parenting as he needs. There is no evidence that the approach you have adopted leads to psychological problems. Thank your friends for their suggestions, chalk them up to differences of opinion, and let it go at that.

infants to facilitate breastfeeding and that fathers also are often present in the beds.

Studies in countries where most adults need regular sleep to maintain fixed work schedules have shown that parents and children alike sleep more soundly in beds of their own. And further studies have shown that children who do not get enough sleep over a prolonged period become irritable and emotional, and find

The notion of medicine to make children sleep is not a new one; opium-based laudanum and homemade concoctions of poppy seeds were widely given to keep babies quiet barely a century ago. Pediatricians now know that medications do not solve children's sleep problems, and even for adults, sleeping pills are at best a temporary fix. Sedative medications change the quality of sleep, making it less restful, and produce a hangover effect the next day. What's more, if a sleep disturbance is the result of habit, sleep medication won't break the cycle. The poor sleeper goes back to his old ways as soon as the medication is stopped; retraining is required to find ways to sleep better.

Certain medications, such as antihistamines for allergies, make children sleepy. Therefore, when prescribed, they should preferably be given at bedtime to prevent drowsiness from affecting daytime activities. Occasionally, the sedative effect of an antihistamine may be a temporary added benefit, if the child has had little sleep due to allergy symptoms. Don't give children any medications or herbal sleep preparations, such as valerian or camomile, without checking with your pediatrician.

it hard to concentrate. These effects can show up in lower test scores by the time children reach school age.

Many advocates of breastfeeding on demand insist that all babies should sleep with their mothers and nurse at will during the night. Some parents prefer this arrangement, while others find that with an extra body in the bed, it's hard to get enough rest. A side-car arrangement—the crib placed next to the parents' bed—may be more comfortable.

For most families, a crib in the parents' room or an adjacent room allows plenty of togetherness with fewer interruptions to sleep. Some families use an intercom to let them listen for sounds from their sleeping infants. In any case, a properly nourished baby does not need night feedings for nourishment after about the first 3 months. Co-sleeping may hamper the child's attempts to develop his own resources for getting to sleep, such as thumb-sucking or cuddling a transitional object.

Safety risks aside, the reasons given for co-sleeping in individual cases may give cause for concern. If the reasons are economic—the parents can't afford a bed for the child—they may benefit from information about financial aid programs. If a parent sleeps with the child to offset loneliness, counseling may be helpful. Occasionally, a co-sleeping child becomes the buffer between partners in a troubled marriage. Again, counseling could help to identify and resolve the problem. If the parents simply prefer to have the child sleep in their bed, they may encounter resistance that requires their pediatrician's intervention when the time inevitably comes to reclaim their bed for themselves and have their child sleep in a bed of her own.

STRATEGIES BEYOND BABYHOOD

When bedtime resistance arises in an older toddler or preschooler, it's often possible to head off trouble by setting up a neutral time-keeper. Put a clock in your child's room, tell her you'll stay with her until "the little hand is on seven and the big hand is on nine" (or whatever time you choose) and pace your going-to-bed routine so that it winds to a close with the clock.

Instead of a clock, your child may enjoy starting an egg timer and watching the sand pass through the glass.

The timekeeper method has a twofold benefit. It's the impartial clock—and not the tired and cranky parent—that says it's time for bed. And it expands your child's understanding of numbers and how they are related to telling time.

Toddlers who have just graduated from a crib to a bed are often intoxicated by the sense of freedom this new status brings. They get into bed willingly enough, then get out again before they've given themselves a chance to become drowsy and start falling asleep. A toddler can easily make twenty or more "farewell

A Three-Year-Old Knows What She's Used To

? *My daughter, who just had her third birthday, will not sleep through the night in her room. She falls asleep in the living room and then we put her into bed. A short time later, she wakes up and wants to go back into the living room.*

Your daughter is comfortable in the living room because that is where she's used to falling asleep. She will enjoy sleeping in her bedroom if she learns to fall asleep there.

Establish a consistent bedtime routine (perhaps stories, hairbrushing, putting toys to bed; see Chapter 6 for suggestions) that takes place entirely in your daughter's room. If there are playthings that she regularly uses in the living room, perhaps they could be moved into the bedroom, too. Tuck your daughter into bed when she's awake and relaxed, say your good nights, and leave the room. If she gets out of bed, try the "odd jobs" (see p. 130) or "in bed—door open, out of bed—door closed" technique (see p. 176). If she wants to be in the living room to stay up with the adults, explain that it's bedtime, and her bedroom is for bedtime while the living room is for daytime. In time, your daughter will form positive sleep associations (see p. 78) in her bedroom and learn to fall asleep there in preference to taking over the living room for sleep.

appearances" in an evening. (For more strategies to deal with bedtime resistance and curtain calls, see Chapter 10.)

Some writers on children's behavior have gone on record instructing parents to hide behind the partly closed bedroom door and keep watch. Then, they say, you jump out and bark, "No climbing out, ever!" as soon as your child makes a move.

With this method, the fright factor might well keep a toddler in bed. He might also lie awake with fear for the rest of the night. A sensitive child could easily develop a nighttime dread of something nasty lurking behind the door—and with good reason. However, you may find it effective to stand watch until your child starts to get out, then gently but firmly say, "No, stay in bed." Some children can simply be told to stay in bed until Mommy or Daddy comes to get them—and they do.

Different children have different temperaments and emotional systems (also see *Sleep and Temperament*, p. 111). As a parent, you will be flooded with advice, whether you ask for it or not, about how to get your child to eat, walk, talk, become potty trained, and sleep. Again, as a parent, you're in the best position to understand your child's needs, according to her temperament.

Thank your friends and relatives for their well-meant suggestions, but take your cues from the one person who knows how to deal with these natural functions: your baby. As you get to know her well, you'll find the ways that suit both of you and that allow her to develop at her own pace.

TIME TO SLEEP

A consistent approach to bedtime may not prevent your baby from waking at night, but it can keep temporary changes in the baby's pattern from developing into a full-scale sleep disorder. From the start, put your baby to sleep in a room that is dark, quiet, and comfortably cool. Avoid rough play and stimulating activities, such as TV and videos, in the hour or so before bedtime. Develop a bedtime routine that emphasizes calm, soothing activities, such as stories and music, in the baby's room, and always bring it to a close by putting your baby still awake into the crib and promptly leaving the room. Ignore cries of protest and give your baby time to settle down, but respond promptly if your baby sounds distressed. When you hear a whimper in the night, give your baby a chance to go back to sleep on his own before checking on him. If he needs attention, give it quietly, keeping the light dim and talking no more than necessary. And remember

PARENTS WITH OPPOSITE POINTS OF VIEW

? *My 2¹/₂-year-old daughter often wakes and cries in the night. After we have calmed her, she stays quiet for a few minutes but then starts crying for us again. My wife wants to let her cry herself back to sleep, but I feel I must go back and calm our little girl by gently rubbing her back. Should we let her cry or is it all right to go back for a few minutes? When she cries, I can't sleep, but my wife says I am setting our daughter up for a lifetime of sleep problems.*

What's important is that you and your wife agree on an approach and join forces to put it into practice. Even if you are not setting your daughter up for a lifetime of sleep troubles, you may unintentionally be giving her the message that "divide and conquer" is a sure path to power. In other words, if Mommy says, "No," go ask Daddy.

Once your toddler is calm and drowsy again, pat her a couple of times and leave the room. When you keep going back as soon as you hear a whimper, you reinforce her crying, instead of helping her comfort herself and fall asleep. Perhaps this is a point where the more objective parent needs to take charge. If you find the crying intolerable, invest in a pair of earplugs and let your wife attend to your daughter's subsequent wakings during the night.

that children are happy and function best when they can look forward to regular schedules for all their needs, including meals, naps, bedtimes, and starting the day's activities.

WHATEVER IT TAKES

During the years from birth to age 5, the one thing parents can count on is change. Young children switch back and forth,

Method	Plus	Minus
Sleep associations (baby put in crib sleepy but awake; parent checks and pats as needed at intervals from 5 to 10 minutes without picking baby up)	✔Baby associates crib and transitional objects with pleasant feeling of falling asleep ✔Easy to use in any family situation ✔Often establishes good sleep habits early on	✘ Baby may find it hard to settle in different surroundings or without transitional objects ✘ May be difficult if child shares room with a sibling, who might be disturbed by comings and goings
Cry it out, also known as Weissbluth method (no going back except in emergency)	✔Baby will fall asleep eventually	✘ With prolonged crying, baby may become too upset to sleep ✘ Can be stressful to hear baby crying for long periods ✘ Noise level may be intolerable if there are other children or home is small
Self-soothing with checking, also known as Ferber method (similar to crying it out but with periodic visits at progressively longer intervals to check without touching baby)	✔Baby learns he's in his crib to stay ✔Parents feel comfortable knowing their child is not seriously distressed	✘ Scheduled visits may get baby's hopes up and provoke further crying ✘ Scheduled intervals longer than 10 minutes may result in distress

Method	Plus	Minus
Scheduled awakenings (parents adapt schedule by awakening baby to cuddle and/or feed before baby's usual waking time)	✔ Parents adapt a schedule so night wakings are less jarring ✔ Can help if there are siblings who are prone to sympathy crying	✘ Disturbs baby's own rhythm unnecessarily ✘ Hard in a single-parent family ✘ Not widely enough practiced to show whether it works for all babies
Co-sleeping, also known as the family bed (child sleeps in parents' bed)	✔ Can facilitate night feedings	✘ Danger of suffocation may outweigh pluses ✘ May unnecessarily prolong night feedings ✘ Neither parent nor child gets adequate sleep ✘ May make it difficult for child to adapt to own bed ✘ Hazardous for young infants because of soft sleep surfaces, loose bedding, and increased risk of SIDS ✘ May mask parental problems that need attention

sleeping through the night for weeks or months at a time, then passing through phases of troubled, fitful nights when the whole family feels cranky because of sleep loss. In the wakeful times, you may feel desperate enough to try everything from leaving your infant in an infant seat or on the floor where she can be lulled by the rhythmical sound of a switched-on clothes dyer, to driving around the neighborhood in the early morning hours with your still-alert toddler enjoying the ride. At these times that try parents' souls, you'll adapt your tactics from night to night and be ready to test almost anything to get your baby to sleep.

As a general rule, however, your baby will settle down with the measures that are woven into your bedtime routine. Like most parents, you will develop a system by trial and error. It may incorporate bits and pieces of several methods, along with advice from your pediatrician and scraps of family lore. Above all, trust your instincts. You know by now what makes your child comfortable. What counts in the end is whether you and your baby get a good night's sleep and wake up refreshed and ready for work and play.

Too many authors of childcare and sleep books, echoing the outdated experts of a century ago, claim to have the one and only solution to every sleep problem. There's rarely a single answer, and different approaches may be needed at various times to help your child over a particular obstacle. For example, we advise that as a rule, children should fall asleep on their own in their own beds. But this rule is occasionally bent or broken in many families without lasting disruption. At one time or another, most parents curl up together with a feverish infant or fearful toddler, and have no difficulty in returning to the normal routine as soon as the episode of illness or nightmares is passed.

Children with special health care needs may have sleep disturbances due to side effects of medication (also see p. 70), breathing problems (see p. 60), or other symptoms. Children who are blind may have disturbances in their biological rhythms that disrupt the sleep cycle. Your pediatrician can advise you about lifestyle changes to manage these problems, and may prescribe medication if necessary to control symptoms or help in adjusting the sleep/wake cycle.

Nightmares and sleep terrors are among the most common causes of sleep disturbance (see Chapter 8). Sleep terrors often appear during the preschool and elementary school years, and nightmares are also frequent in school-age children. Accepting that they are part of normal development, or knowing that other family members have had them, can ease the anxiety that these events bring. Reassurance and comfort are usually all that's needed. Most youngsters grow out of these conditions after the

"BUT IF YOU TRY SOMETIMES, YOU GET WHAT YOU NEED"

In today's increasingly typical household, where both parents work outside the home, setting regular bedtimes for children can be challenging. Youngsters and parents alike want to spend time together and share the events of the day.

For toddlers and preschoolers, it's fairly simple to adjust naptimes and allow for going to bed later, after the parents return home. But once children are on fixed school schedules, problems arise if late bedtimes mean daytime drowsiness. If something's got to give, it may have to be the nightly time together. Try to make up for the loss on weeknights by having extra time together on the weekends.

early years of childhood.

Changes in diet can cause sleep changes. If your child is having frequent broken nights, try giving the main meal earlier and avoid foods with a high calorie content in the evening hours immediately before bed. However, a drink of water, or of warm milk before brushing the teeth, may be a soothing part of the bedtime routine (for more about foods and sleep, see pp. 71–74).

Regardless of any advice you may be offered, you will discover the approaches that work not only for your family, but for each child within your family. What works for one may not help another; much depends on the child's temperament (see p. 111), birth order, and the family dynamics. Thoughtful parents mistrust experts who insist that one technique works for all children all the time, with no exceptions. Such rigid techniques applied to sleeping, eating, and other natural functions can evolve into tools for controlling children, rather than encouraging youngsters to develop as individuals with their own internal systems of behavioral checks and balances.

CHAPTER 6

Bedtime Routines
and Rituals

Four-year-old Katie's mother never varied the schedule: dinner at 6 P.M., bath at 6:30, play for 15 minutes, then lights out by 7:15, sleepy or not. She was becoming increasingly impatient with Katie's repeated requests for drinks of water, having the door a little more open or a little more closed, and questions about this and that.

Across town, Dylan, a preschool playmate of Katie's, stayed asleep where he dropped off, generally in front of the TV. His mother had long since given up nightly struggles to get Dylan to settle into bed, and preferred to save her energy for the inevitable morning rush. She kept the peace by simply covering him with a comforter where he lay.

It's almost impossible to overstress the importance of a calm, orderly bedtime routine, but we don't want to suggest that parents should set a fixed routine and stick to it, no matter what. Perhaps we should talk about bedtime routines, rather than a routine.

Katie's mother was needlessly strict about scheduling; Katie wasn't ready to sleep at 7:15. Allowed another 30 minutes or so for reading and quiet play, she would more easily settle for sleep and make fewer "curtain calls." By contrast, Dylan's mother had never really tried to get Dylan into a regular going-to-bed routine and, instead, let the TV do the job for her. It's not too late to change a poor habit and help Dylan to get ready for bed with quiet time in his bedroom. By keeping the evenings more orderly, the family could avoid the troublesome morning rush.

START WITH A ROUTINE

Your going-to-bed procedure may vary slightly from day to day, depending on how tired and ready for bed your child feels; however, the basic elements should always be the same. Sometimes, you may skip the bedtime routine altogether, except for a clean-up, change, and good night kiss, when your child is exhausted after a long and action-packed day. Mostly, however, you'll find time to wind down, usually beginning with a warm, relaxing bath, and leading into a quiet chat, music and stories, saying goodnight to the family pets, putting toys to bed, and—if it's your family's way—saying prayers. Avoid scary stories and games involving monster chases or other activities that may be overstimulating. Turn off the TV and videos in the hour or so before bedtime and keep interactions calm and soothing

AFTER BABYHOOD. As children grow out of babyhood, they can start the bedtime routine by helping with a quick clean-up to put toys and books back in their places and leave the room tidy for the morning. Bedtime also brings lots of opportunities for thoughtful one-on-one talks. However, it is not the time to raise issues that may make your youngster anxious, such as reproaches for bad behavior or a poor school report.

Even though certain parts of the routine, such as stories or games, may vary from one night to another, it's essential that the "indispensable" steps always be included. Brush your child's teeth or help her to brush them. (Most children need close supervision and help with brushing and flossing until they are about 8 years old. And for a long time afterward, parents may have to remind youngsters to brush their teeth every night and morning until it becomes second nature.) Remind her to use the bathroom one last time if she is toilet trained or even if she is still learning to be dry at night. Perhaps give her a small drink of water if it's something she needs in order to settle down.

With bedtime activities, as with other aspects of behavior such

GAGGING AND THROWING UP: PROVEN SCARE TACTICS

? *My son, age 2 1/2, has always gone to sleep with either Mom or Dad lying beside him. Now we're trying to break the habit and get him to go to bed by himself. The problem is, he cries to the point of gagging and almost throws up. Help!*

We don't recommend that you leave your toddler to cry until he's too worked up to sleep. However, gagging and throwing up are not harmful in themselves, and some toddlers deliberately gag and make vomiting sounds because they know it's a shortcut to parental attention. A few episodes of minor gagging and throwing up may be an inconvenience you have to put up with to help your child reach the important goal of settling by himself. To make clean-ups quick and easy, put two sheets on the mattress, so you can whisk the soiled one away without having to remake the bed.

Keep this necessary transition period less upsetting for your child by following a regular bedtime routine. Try the "odd job" method of gradual withdrawal (see p. 130), or sit quietly either in your child's room or in a chair just outside the door, where he can still see you as he becomes sleepy. You may have to follow the same procedure several nights in a row, perhaps moving your chair farther from your child's bed and closer to the door (also see p. 139) until the new habit becomes an established one.

as eating and toilet training, let your child take the initiative. If she suggests a reasonable change in the routine, you've nothing to gain by insisting on doing things your way. Your job is to monitor events, making sure that any changes are in the direction of calming rather than stimulating, and keeping an eye on the clock. Like a benevolent ruler, you are there to advise and to warn, occa-

"IF IT AIN'T BROKE, DON'T FIX IT"

? *My 2-year-old likes to lie in bed and look at her books until very late. I try to take the books away but then she cries for hours. She is very stubborn and won't give up! I won't go to sleep before she does, so I keep checking on her until I'm sure she's asleep. What should I do?*

Your daughter is attached to her books. When you remove them, you are taking away transitional objects that comfort her and help her relax in preparation for sleep. Let your toddler have her books; they keep her quiet and content. Remove them after she's asleep if they clutter up the bed. There's no need either to keep checking on your child or to wait up until she goes to sleep. If she needs you in the night, she'll call for attention.

sionally to consent, and now and again to veto. One sleep expert put it this way:

> The challenge is to establish comfortable, effective routines which should achieve a happy compromise between the disorder and confusion that can occur without them and the rigidity and boredom that can come with too much structure and regimentation, where children are given no choice and little flexibility.

In other words, be consistent but know when to bend the rules.

EARLY CHILDHOOD: WHEN DOES A ROUTINE BEGIN?

It's never too soon to begin developing a going-to-bed routine. From the time your baby is brand new, waking for feedings every two or three hours, it's good to establish a rhythm. During the daylight hours, enjoy increasingly longer periods of wakefulness, talk, and play, and bring the day to a close with a nightly ritual:

Toddlers suck their thumbs and cuddle transitional objects—soft toys, blankets—to comfort themselves as they fall asleep. In time, merely sucking the thumb or holding the object may be enough to soothe a youngster into a drowsy state. A child who can "find" her thumb or fingers to suck will soon lull herself to sleep. However, many children need a little help in settling on a transitional object, or "lovey." Place a small, soft toy in the crib where it's the last thing your child sees at night and the first in the morning. As she becomes better coordinated and more mobile, she'll look for it and play with it to comfort herself.

If your infant is fretful at bedtime, a pacifier may help. However, if you use a pacifier, be prepared to have to get up when it falls out of your baby's mouth and she can't find it on her own. You will have to act as a willing retriever until your baby has the coordination to feel for it and put it back in her mouth. No matter how many times you have to rescue the pacifier, the American Academy of Pediatrics warns:

Do not attempt to solve this problem by tying a pacifier to your child's crib, or around your child's neck or hand. This is very dangerous and could cause serious injury or even death.

Wash your baby's face, hands, and bottom; change her into sleep clothes; brush her hair; and rock or cuddle her while singing or listening to quiet music before placing her, still awake, in her crib.

Even though your baby may awaken for a feeding only a few hours later and will continue to wake up for night feedings for some time, this rhythm helps her to learn that daytime is for waking and nighttime for sleeping. The way you feed her reinforces the message: daytime feedings in bright light, followed by play then a nap; nighttime feedings in dim light, ending with a prompt return to bed in a darkened room.

Problems with separation anxiety tend to loom larger with firstborn and only children. The greater frequency and intensity are often blamed on the parents' overeagerness to do the right thing mingled with worry over their inexperience. However, there's another side to the story. First and only children tend to suffer more intense separation anxiety because they feel themselves to be part of a unit with the parents. It's only natural to be frightened of separations that threaten to break up that unit. In a child's mind, going to sleep is one such separation.

When the second child appears on the scene, it's easier for the first one to understand his place in the family and develop notions of activities and behaviors that are appropriate for children versus adults. And second and later-born children usually—but not always—have less intense anxiety about separation because they are bolstered by the constant presence of the older sibling. (Also see *Sleep and Temperament,* p. 111.)

Starting at about 8 weeks, your baby may enjoy listening and watching as you describe what's going on in a picture book. At this age, she is far from being able to follow a story, but you both will enjoy the shared closeness. In this way, you prepare for story reading later on and begin to help your child develop the priceless habit of paying attention.

CRYING BEFORE SLEEP. For some babies, crying seems to be a way to work off energy as they settle down to sleep, and a means of becoming fully alert when they awaken. A baby who wails loudly the moment his parents leave the bedroom may just be saying good night. Left to cry it out, he won't continue wailing for hours. Instead, he'll probably cry and fuss for a few minutes, then soothe himself with his thumb, pacifier, or whatever may comfort him, and drift into sleep. On the other hand, starting about the middle of the first year, the cause may be separation anxiety. If he does keep on fussing, the best way to deal with it is to pop your head in the doorway every 5 minutes or so and quietly repeat your usual sign-off, be it "good night" or "sleep tight." This lets your baby know that you're nearby, but that fun and games are over: It's time to go to sleep. In the daytime, play peek a boo and similar games to teach your baby that "gone away" doesn't always mean "gone forever."

By the same token, if your baby cries and fusses on waking in the morning, he may not want attention right away. Give him a little while to wake up on his own. He may calm down, sing or babble to himself, and play quietly for a while. Then, if he makes a more insistent cry, take it as a signal that he's ready to get up.

SLEEP DIARY

When bedtime refusals or other sleep problems persist despite treatment efforts, including a consistent going-to-bed routine, it's helpful to keep a sleep diary for a week or two. Some pediatricians ask parents to keep a sleep diary as an aid to the diagnosis of sleep problems. Parents use the diary to jot down daily answers to the following questions:

- What did we do during our bedtime routine?

- How long did the bedtime routine last?

- What time did the child actually get into bed and settle down to sleep?

- How long did she cry after the parents left the room?

- How many "curtain calls" (requests for drinks...extra hugs...toilet) were there before settling?

- How many awakenings were there during the night?

- What steps did the parents take to deal with awakenings and curtain calls?

The sleep diary helps both the parents and their pediatrician pinpoint aspects of behavior that need attention. It also helps to identify minor problems that are likely to fade away if left alone.

Farther up the Ladder: Routines in the School Years

For school-age children, a quick tidy-up is part of the bedtime routine: putting books and toys back on shelves, clothes in drawers and closets. The room doesn't have to be perfect, but it's more pleasant to rest and read or listen to music and stories in a tidy environment, and mornings go more smoothly if needed objects are where they belong and thus easy to find.

By the middle-school years, the weekend routine is a bit less regimented than the one for school nights, and weekend bedtimes can be later. However, while your child may sleep late the next morning, try to keep weekend wake-ups within an hour or so of the usual time, especially if your child is not a creature of habit by nature. Left to sleep too long, in only a few days a vulnerable child can shift his sleep phase (periods of waking and sleeping) in such a way that he has trouble getting back on his usual schedule. School performance may suffer because he is drowsy.

No More "Just One More"

A parent who spends the day apart from his child is a soft target for pleas of "just one more" story or game or other nighttime activity. As with settling a fussy, crying infant, the going-to-bed routine for older children may work more smoothly if the parent who is less susceptible to pressure takes charge.

Setting Limits

Children are less likely to develop problems of resistance when their parents set firm, fair limits. This applies to going to bed just as it does to other areas of behavior. Enjoy your evening playtime with your child, but bring it to an end when bedtime rolls around. Make it a rule that once it's time for sleep, she's to stay in bed until morning. If she isn't sleepy, let her have a favorite toy or book to pass the time in her bed or crib. Bedtime is bedtime, after all, even if it's not quite sleeptime. Of course, you must make exceptions and allow your child out when she needs a change or clean-up, comfort after a bad dream, or attention for symptoms such as a fever or vomiting.

KEEPING ROUTINES MANAGEABLE

Unless carefully managed, bedtime routines can be drawn out almost indefinitely, thus defeating the purpose for which they're intended. A child quickly learns that by taking charge of the show, she can significantly delay the time of going to bed. For example, she may have repeatedly to switch her stuffed animals because she can't find quite the right combination to make her sleepy on a particular night. She may invoke heaven's blessings on a list of names that approaches the length of a telephone directory. Or she may desperately need the answers to questions that will keep her awake if she has to wait until morning.

Allow your child flexibility within the routine, but keep things under your control by limiting the choices available. For example, let her choose different stuffed animals for her bed each night, but keep her to a fixed number. Let her choose a story and a song, but not a whole book or CD.

SLEEP AND TEMPERAMENT

Temperament, or behavioral style, is among the most important factors in determining first, how children and parents will react in a given situation, and second, how parents teach and care for their children. A baby's basic temperament—be he easy-going or touchy, calm or irritable—usually begins to be evident in the first weeks of life. It strongly influences the way the caregiver looks after the baby. It also has a major bearing on the way the child develops regular routines, including sleep schedules. Despite the vast range of variations in temperament, a true mismatch between child and parent is very rare. And although definitive studies have not been done, mismatches among adoptive parents and their

DRAW THE LINE

? *Our 3-year-old son refuses to sleep alone and instead goes to bed with me and my husband between 9:30 and 10:00 most nights. Our 6-year-old daughter has no problem going to her own bed on time at 8:00 P.M., but in the middle of the night she also squeezes in with the rest of us.*

Sleeping on his own is not my son's only problem, or rather, my problem. He refuses to fall asleep; keeps telling me he wants to play; wants me to get up and watch a video or TV with him; and often yells—until our ears are ringing—that he does not want lights out. This is hard because I need to get up at 5:00 A.M. to be at work by 7:00. My son also refuses to take scheduled naps; he only naps when his eyes literally close. If his sitter tries to put him to bed during the day, he screams that he doesn't want to nap, he wants to play.

How can we help our children not be afraid of sleeping on their own?

Children are happiest when they know who's in charge and what their limits are. Your son, at 3, is far too young to know what's best for himself or the family; however, because he's unsure of how far he can go, he constantly tests the boundaries. It's time to lay down some rules and enforce them. You and your husband must agree on a plan and keep to it. In doing so, you will not only help your children to sleep better, but you will also teach them to consider other people's needs and feelings. Unless you do this, your son may have a difficult time getting on with playmates, adjusting to school, and eventually, dealing with life in the wide world.

First, tell your children that from now on, everybody

sleeps in his or her own bed. This will let all the family get the sleep you need to work and have fun in the daytime. When your children get up at night, stay calm and lead them back to their own beds. Remember, your son will welcome even negative attention as a reward, so don't get upset, silently count to 10 if it helps, and keep your interaction with him on a low and unemotional level.

Second, set up new rules for TV/video watching and computer games, allowing a maximum of 1 to 2 hours a day, and in the daytime only. Select the programs your children watch, filter out violent shows and games, and choose materials suitable for your children's age group. Move the set to an inconvenient location—the basement or garage—if necessary to enforce the new policy.

Third, when your son wants to play at night, tell him it's not playtime, it's sleeptime. Let him have a book and one or two soft toys to play with quietly in his bed. Leave a night-light in his room and try the "in bed—door open, out of bed—door closed" method (see p. 176) to keep him in his room. (However, before you go to bed, shut the doors to all sleeping rooms. The American Academy of Pediatrics recommends that doors to sleeping rooms be kept shut at night as a fire safety measure.) Make sure that your child's room is "childproof"—free of breakable or hazardous objects.

In making these changes, you may endure several nights of noise and disruption, but if you are calm and consistent, your children will accept the new rules and your whole family will enjoy better sleep and a more pleasant and restful atmosphere.

Finally, don't be afraid to set limits; your children are asking for them. Your pediatrician may provide information about parent-effectiveness training; many schools, churches, and temples sponsor such programs for developing parenting skills.

COMMONSENSE GUIDELINES FOR SETTLING DOWN AT BEDTIME

DON'T	DO
✗ Let your baby fall asleep at the breast or bottle.	✔ Place your child in her crib or bed sleepy but still awake.
✗ Leave your baby with a bottle in bed; this practice can promote ear infections and tooth decay.	✔ Finish bottle-feeding out of bed.
✗ Roughhouse in the hour before bedtime.	✔ Play gently.
✗ Tell scary or sad stories.	✔ Read cheerful stories with happy endings.
✗ Allow TV and videos in the hour before bedtime.	✔ Turn off TV and videos; sing or play relaxing music.
✗ Give large drinks and heavy snacks just before bedtime.	✔ Allow a small drink of water or warm milk, light snacks such as cereal, crackers and cheese, yogurt, or fruit. Brush teeth before settling down for the night.
✗ Rush into your child's room at the first sound you hear.	✔ Unless you hear a cry of real distress, give your child a few minutes to settle back to sleep on her own.

children appear to be no more frequent than mismatches among biological parents and their offspring.

However, although the seeds of temperament are in our genes, temperament is not a fixed characteristic, as gender is. It is modified by many influences in the environment. Some inborn aspects of temperament may take years to emerge, as do certain other genetic traits that are activated in stages. With time, children learn to fit into society by modifying the temperamental characteristics that affect their relationships with others. For example, a naturally shy child may work to overcome his reticence or, conversely, may exaggerate it if he is comfortable with the negative attention it attracts. Finally, behavior and temperament can undergo temporary changes under the influence of medications, such as those used to improve concentration in attention deficit disorder, or drugs such as alcohol. The behavioral effects of medications and drugs generally disappear once the substance has passed out of the body.

Temperament influences the way sleep habits are organized and maintained through a three-way effect on interactions between the child and her parents or caregivers. First, it affects the way the parent responds to the child's demands. Second, it affects the impact of environmental factors on the child. And third, it affects the way the child responds to the care provided. One sleep expert has noted, "It is often difficult to determine whether disturbed sleep was caused initially by a specific temperament trait or by a parent's behavior...because interactive effects always evolve." Temperamental interactions may cause many different sleep problems. For instance, if parents respond irregularly to a child with low natural rhythmicity (see next page), the sleep schedule is likely to be erratic. Parents who are oversolicitous, in a well-meaning effort to meet their child's needs, may unwittingly set up a vicious cycle of night waking and crying in a child with an intense, irritable temperament. And a child who is naturally persistent may regularly delay bedtime to unreasonable lengths if her parents don't know how to say "No" (see *Keeping Routines Manageable*, p. 111). Regardless of the specifics of the case, the result is always the same: The child doesn't get enough sleep, is inattentive and learns poorly at school, and develops a stress response that makes her overaroused, more difficult, and more emotional.

If this sounds like a problem that may be growing in your

Psychologists examine nine major characteristics in evaluating children's temperament:

- Activity level—the amount of physical activity, restlessness, or fidgety behavior that a child shows in daily activities (and that may affect sleep).

- Rhythmicity or regularity—the ability to develop a regular pattern for natural functions, including eating, sleeping, and bowel habits.

- Approach and withdrawal—the way a child responds to new stimuli, such as people, places, foods, and changes to the normal routine.

- Adaptability—the ease or difficulty with which a child adapts to change.

- Intensity—the energy level or intensity, happiness or unhappiness, that a child shows in responding to a situation.

- Mood—the degree of pleasantness expressed in a child's words and behavior.

- Attention span—the ability to concentrate or stay with a task (both under- and over-persistence may be negative traits, depending on other personality features).

- Distractibility—the ease with which a child can be distracted from a task by stimuli in the environment.

- Sensory threshold—the amount of stimulation required to evoke a distinct response from a child (some children respond to slight stimulation, others require more intense levels for arousal).

family, ask your pediatrician for an impartial evaluation of the situation. Referral to a family therapist may be helpful, and your pediatrician may be able to put you in touch with a support group for parents and children with similar problems.

Although individual cases require specific measures, pediatricians recommend a few general strategies to help parents and children overcome temperamental difficulties:

1. Set up a neutral emotional climate for dealing with your child. Make an effort not to respond emotionally and instinctively, which is usually unproductive.

2. Try not to take your child's behavior personally. Many of the characteristics you find upsetting are inborn and he is not deliberately being annoying. Avoid blaming him or yourself.

3. Set priorities on the issues affecting your child. Deal with the most pressing ones first, then with the rest in order; some may disappear before you get around to them.

4. Deal with problems in the present moment; avoid "What ifs?" and try not to look far into the future.

5. Take an objective look at your own temperament and behavior and try to put yourself in your child's shoes. Perhaps you could find ways to adjust your style to foster a better fit with your child.

6. Anticipate situations where conflict is likely to occur and try to head them off or keep the impact to a minimum. When problems can't be avoided altogether, accept the possibility that the day may be difficult and be prepared to make the best of it.

7. Ask yourself whether your expectations for your child are realistic. Take every opportunity to praise her for tasks she does right and reinforce the behaviors that you like.

While misunderstandings can occur in any family, true temperamental mismatches, giving rise to constant conflict, are quite rare. Successful families are those whose members appreciate and respect one another's temperamental differences and do their best to get along with one another.

Children tend to have more frequent sleep disturbances after their parents separate or divorce. In young children, this increase is due to a surge in separation anxiety stemming from fear of abandonment by both parents. "After all," the child may reason, "if one parent has left our home for good, what's to keep the other from doing the same?"

Whether you're the custodial or noncustodial parent, each time you leave your child in the care of another person, let her know when you'll be back or when you expect to speak with her next: "I'll pick you up next Friday at 6:00," or "Call me before you leave for school tomorrow." If you don't know the exact time, give a guideline: "I'll be home in time for dinner," or "I'll be back tonight but not until after you're in bed so let's talk tomorrow morning."

Remember that children can deal with disappointing news, but lack of information worries them and stimulates their imagination. Indeed, the fewer facts they have to work with, the more elaborate their imaginary explanations are likely to be. Left to figure situations out for themselves, children tend to fear the worst.

SLEEP DISTURBANCES AFTER SEPARATION OR DIVORCE

It can be difficult to maintain consistent bedtimes and going-to-bed routines when your child divides her time between two homes after a separation or divorce. When custody involves regular weekend and holiday visits to the noncustodial parent, changes in the routine are usually taken in stride like other exceptions to a basic schedule. However, in an inherently stressful situation a youngster may regress to more babyish or "childish" behavior, at least for a while. Thumb-sucking and bed-wetting may recur or appear for the first time in a preschooler or school-age child; night fears may make it hard to settle for sleep. An older child or adolescent may act withdrawn, defiant, or over-eager to please. Sleep disturbances—either insomnia or oversleeping—are common in youngsters under emotional stress.

KEEPING A CONSISTENT BEDTIME ROUTINE IN TWO HOMES. Problems tend to be more difficult to deal with when the child is required to make frequent changes, perhaps spending a few days of the week at one parent's home and the rest at the other's. Sleep disorders, with bedtime refusals and nighttime wakings, are common among children who feel torn between two parents, two homes, and two different routines.

Problems may arise out of conflict due to widely different styles in the two homes, regardless of the custody arrangements. In an extreme case, a perfectionist parent who allows no flexibility at all in schedules for meals and bedtimes may be pitched against the former partner, who lets the children snack without restraint and go to sleep where they drop in front of the TV. A person would have to be an emotional quick-change artist to make such a demanding about-face every few days. Yet many youngsters are asked to do just that; the child has no sooner adapted to one home when she must adjust to the other. Difficulties arise out of irregularity in routines and lack of cooperation between the parents. It takes unusually close teamwork between the two parents to make an arrangement work—perhaps even closer than when they lived under one roof.

FOSTERING SELF-RELIANCE. One way to deal with such difficulties might be to step back and take a relatively minor role in your child's bedtime routine. Of course, this can't be done at the toddler stage, when your child needs lots of help with dressing, washing, using the potty, and winding-down diversions such as stories. When your child is somewhat older, however, it's possible to take advantage of bedtime to foster her self-reliance. Provide props to take your place when you can't be around. Equip her with a cassette player and tape library so she can listen to favorite stories and songs when she's preparing for bed, no matter which parent she's staying with. Let her keep duplicates of especially favorite bedtime toys and books at both homes to prevent problems due to haste or forgetfulness.

Once the family's situation has stabilized, sleep problems and other symptoms should gradually disappear over several weeks. If they persist, talk to your pediatrician, who may suggest a referral for counseling and possibly participation in a support group.

NIGHT OWLS

YOUNG CHILDREN. There are children—even toddlers and preschoolers—who take a long time to get to sleep after a regular going-to-bed routine, despite their own and their parents' best efforts. Some find it hard to lie quietly for long periods in the dark. It's often easier for them to get drowsy if they can slip out of bed and quietly prowl about for a while. They may eventually drop off to sleep on the floor. In almost all cases, these children also wake up later in the morning, are hard to rouse, and tend to be cranky for some time after being awakened.

If your child is one of these night owls, insist that although he may get out of bed, he must stay in his room. Leave on a nightlight for safety but don't allow other lights. A safety gate across the bedroom doorway may be necessary to reinforce your message. Even a child who can climb over barriers will respect a gate, provided your instructions are clear and firm. When you find your child asleep on his bedroom floor, put him into bed. At least he'll be used to waking up in bed and in time he'll accept that bed is a comfortable place for going to sleep, as well.

SHIFTING THE SLEEP PHASE. One way to solve your night owl's problem may be to shift his sleep phase (see p. 26) so that he feels tired and goes to sleep earlier. However, shifting the sleep phase is not always easy and it cannot be done in a single step. If you put your child to bed at 7:00 P.M. when he is used to falling asleep at 10:00, he will have to endure hours of wakefulness and possibly boredom. This is unlikely to make him enjoy being in bed; instead, he may view his bed as a place of punishment rather than a comfortable refuge.

It's better to use a gradual approach. Start with the time your child usually falls asleep as your baseline and work back with a quarter-hour change about every 3 or 4 nights until your child has reprogrammed his pattern and is now sleepy at the bedtime you want. For example, if he regularly drops off at 10:00 P.M., start your new schedule by putting him to bed for the first night or two at 10:00 as usual. Then, for the next 3 or 4 nights, put him to bed at 9:45. By the final night, he should be adjusted to getting sleepy at the new time. Continue the reprogramming with a 15-minute change every 3 or 4 days until your child is ready for bed at your target bedtime. One month is usually long enough for the adjustment. If you hit a snag at any quarter-hour stage during the process, don't give up or go back. Spend a few more days at the latest level you've reached, then restart the process with that time as your new baseline.

The wake-up time is more important than the bedtime in shifting the sleep phase and regulating circadian rhythms. As you adjust your child's schedule, keep to a single wake-up time and do not vary it, even on weekends.

SUGGESTED SCHEDULE FOR REPROGRAMMING A NIGHT OWL

NIGHTS	BEDTIMES
1–2	10:00 P.M.
3–5	9:45 P.M.
6–8	9:30 P.M.
9–11	9:15 P.M.
12–14	9:00 P.M.
15–17	8:45 P.M.
18–20	8:30 P.M.
21–23	8:15 P.M.
24–26	8:00 P.M.

STAYING UP LATE

On special holidays and family celebrations even the youngest members of the family get to stay up late. This means they may miss out on the usual bedtime routine. A child who stays up way past bedtime may become overtired and grouchy after a day full of fun. In this frame of mind he may have trouble relaxing for sleep. A shortened version of your bedtime routine—one song, one story, one animal to hug—may do the trick.

Lots of family outings end with children falling asleep in the car on the way home and being carried to bed without waking. Youngsters often sleep better if you anticipate these events where possible by washing them, changing them into sleep clothes, and brushing teeth before leaving for home. There are sleep experts who insist that once home, you should wake your child and put him through the usual routine. However, more moderate voices counsel otherwise. Unless you are dealing with a youngster whose unusually rigid, compulsive personality adapts poorly to change, it's not worth waking a sleeping child just to go through the motions of a bedtime routine. Let sleeping dogs and children lie.

Vacations and Sleepovers

The key to having the whole family sleep well on vacations is to temper the novelty of a new environment with some of the familiar sensations that your child finds comforting. Of course, you wouldn't leave home without "teddy" or "ducky"—whoever the favorite companion may be. You may also play it safe by taking the blanket and pillow your child is used to. But even if your child is an infant, don't underestimate her willingness to get into the vacation spirit and enjoy a change of surroundings. A youngster who is used to a regular routine at home generally adapts well to change, because she remains confident that her needs will be met, no matter where she finds herself.

Whatever your child's age may be, during vacations, try to keep her on her normal sleep/wake schedule. If the vacation involves travel to a different time-zone, adopt local time from the moment you arrive, but be prepared to allow for naps at odd times to make up for sudden onsets of fatigue. As soon as you get home, switch back immediately to your regular time. Children are adaptable. Once your youngster gets back to her usual schedule for play, meals, and sleep, any disturbance in her sleep/wake cycle will probably disappear within a few days.

SPRING FORWARD, FALL BACK

Changes for daylight saving time in the spring and fall may disrupt your child's sleeping patterns for a few days after the clocks are reset. When the clocks move forward an hour in the spring, bedtime is an hour earlier and your youngster will still be wide awake. He may take a long time to become drowsy. It's a mistake to try to compensate by changing his bedtime. This only prolongs the period required for adaptation. Keep to the usual bedtimes and wake-ups by the clock to make the adjustment smoother.

Again, when clocks are turned back an hour in the fall, no special measures need be taken. Your child will probably be tired before the clock says it's time for bed. It won't do any harm to let him get ready for bed a little earlier than usual. He may also wake a bit earlier for the first few days, but will soon be back on track provided you follow a regular timetable.

If you run into difficulties on either side of the change, try the 15-minute schedule suggested in *Shifting the Sleep Phase*, p. 120. Also, check the light level in your child's bedroom and make any necessary adjustments by installing window coverings or adding an extra lamp. Prolonged light in the evenings may make it hard to fall asleep for some children, just as darkness in the mornings may make it harder to get up.

EARLY BIRDS

Just when you thought you had settled into a good nighttime routine, your child starts waking up, ready to rise and shine an hour or two before the rest of the family. Some youngsters wake up because they have had enough sleep and are naturally early risers. Other children wake up prematurely, before they've had the right amount of sleep. Often, the cause is something in the environment, such as bright early morning light, the sound of a

WAKING TOO EARLY

 My 5-year-old gets up too early. His bedtime is 9:00 P.M. (changed from 8:00 in an effort to delay his waking) and he wakes up between 4:00 and 5:00 A.M. By noon he's tired out. Unfortunately, he was assigned to a kindergarten class that begins at 12:30. He's irritable and sometimes behaves disruptively, and usually wants to take a nap in the middle of class. We've installed dark shades in his room (it's still dark when he wakes, anyway) and we don't know what else to do. Should we keep him up even later?

Buy an inexpensive clock-radio for your son's room and set it for 7:00 A.M. (or any time you choose). Tell your son that from now on, he must stay in his bed until the radio switches on and the numbers read 7:00. He may play with toys in bed or browse through a book if he wakes early, but he may not turn on any lights apart from the night-light, or leave his bed except to use the bathroom. If there's a TV or VCR in his room, move it out. Go to his room, if you must, to make sure that the lights are off and he is in bed, according to the new rules.

Go back to an 8:00 P.M. bedtime, but allow for a regular winding-down routine, including listening to stories or quiet music but no TV or videos, before lights out at 8:45 or 9:00.

If you follow this schedule consistently for several weeks, your son's sleep phase (the hours spent asleep out of the 24) should shift until he is returning to sleep after his early waking. Eventually he may remain asleep until the alarm goes off. However, you must be prepared to accept the fact that your son may be a naturally early riser—perhaps the only lark in a family of owls—who also needs less sleep than the other members of the family.

neighbor's car starting up at the same time each morning, or the discomfort of a cold, sodden diaper.

You will have an idea whether your child is getting enough sleep by the way he behaves throughout the day. If he's irritable and lacking energy, or needs to sleep within one to two hours after waking, he's probably not sleeping long enough. Of course, if your child is unusually tired, you should also check for symptoms—such as fever, pallor, or lack of appetite—indicating that he may need medical attention. Most toddlers function best on 9 to 10 hours of sleep a night, plus daytime naps. If your child is

LARKS VS. OWLS

The differences between so-called larks and owls involve more than just the times for getting up and going to bed. Thanks to the circadian rhythms governing hormone secretion and temperature regulation, owls are always at their best and most alert late in the evening and always have trouble getting up and on the go in the morning, no matter how long they have slept. And for larks, of course, the opposite is true. However, although very early waking can be a problem with young children, few parents worry about a lark who goes to sleep at a reasonable hour and wakes up bright-eyed and ready for action.

If you have an owl-child in your family, he may find it difficult to fall asleep at the bedtime you've set, even when you keep to a strict schedule. Luckily, although many adults fall into this pattern, children are somewhat more adaptable. Although they may be wakeful for some time after going to bed, they generally have fewer problems falling asleep than adults do.

It's important to maintain an owl on the same daily schedule for waking, even on weekends, to prevent the circadian rhythms from shifting steadily later. Keep your child's bedtime routines calm and unhurried, and let sleep associations induce a feeling of relaxation leading to drowsiness.

getting less than this amount, you may need to take steps to help him sleep longer and more restfully.

If early sunlight is waking your child sooner than necessary, install shades or curtains to keep the bedroom dark. Noise from inside or outside the house can often be covered up with white noise from an electric fan or even a tape recording. Heavy curtains may also help. Early waking caused by clammy, oversoaked diapers may stop if you switch to ultra-absorbent diapers or pull-ups designed for nighttime use.

You may be the parent of a naturally early riser. If your child is also early-to-bed and regularly sleeps the same number of hours every night—always tucked in by, say, 7:30 P.M. and waking at 5 A.M.—you may be able to reset her wake-up time by encouraging her to stay up a bit later (perhaps in 15-minute increments, as recommended in the schedule on p. 121). However, if you are unwilling to trade some of your free time in the evenings for more of your child's company, help her to understand that although she may be awake, others need to sleep longer. Therefore, she must learn to play quietly in her room without disturbing the family until it's time to get up. Place a selection of toys and books within reach. Perhaps leave a digital clock-radio by her bed and explain that when the radio switches on or the numbers read 6:45 (or any other time you may choose) it's time to call Mommy or Daddy. If your early riser "forgets" that she must stay in her room, install a gate that she can't climb over in her doorway.

CHAPTER 7

There's a Monster
Under the Bed:
Dealing with Fears

"See, there's nothing to be afraid of," Matthew's mother said as she opened the closet door wide and shone a flashlight. "It's just your imagination. Now sleep tight."

The next night, 3-year-old Matthew called out, "You'd better get in here, Mommy. My imagination's back in the closet again!"

Separation anxiety makes for frequent broken nights starting in the latter half of the first year and gradually fading away about the second birthday. At night, the preschooler's vivid imagination emerges as fear of the dark or of monsters that may or may not seem to have direct connection with the exposures and experiences of daily life: In some cases, fears can be linked directly to TV programs, including the news.

By school age, imaginary threats give way to more realistic fears, often involving bodily harm, kidnapping, or intruders. A new onset of bedtime fears

*F*ears and worries are normal for even the most well-adjusted child. Indeed, different stages of development are marked by certain clearly defined fears. As early as 5 months, for example, a baby may appear wary when confronted with an unfamiliar face. What's hard for parents to understand is that when the cause can be identified, the fear seems to be out of all proportion to what triggered it. Interestingly, similar triggers can set off fears in children the same age, no matter whether they appear to have fearful or "fearless" personalities.

Fairy Tales—Perhaps Not for the Average Young Child

Fairy tales, most of which originated in ancient times as entertainment for adults to pass the evenings, are notorious for triggering frightening images in young imaginations at bedtime. The moral lessons they convey, while valid and timeless, are often couched in earthy parables that are hard for young minds to break down and absorb. For children of any age who are prone to fears and nightmares, choose reading material carefully and avoid challenging tales that may conjure up scary images after dark.

often coincides with a normal separation, such as starting out of home care. Unusual stresses also bring out fears: for example, moving to a new house, the arrival of a new baby, or a mother's switch to full-time work outside the home. No matter how far-fetched they may seem, fears are normal and protective; they teach caution and hold children back from taking needless risks. Only in unusual cases do fears become so overwhelming that they interfere with children's development.

At some time, most children have recurrent episodes of fearfulness that disrupt sleep. Fears are often at the root of the most

Typical Fears at Different Developmental Stages

Infancy	Loud noises, falling, separation from parents, strange faces, sensory overload
Preschool	Animals, the dark, separation, imaginary monsters, going to school (change; fear of the unknown)
School years and adolescence	Family fights, punishment, social rejection, not performing well (school, sports), war, school violence, crime, family concerns, issues related to sexual development

common sleep problems: resistance at bedtime, trouble falling asleep, and nightmares (for more about nightmares and sleep terrors, see Chapter 8). Although fears may upset children at any age, psychologists have charted two normal peaks in the frequency and intensity of fears that follow the resolution of separation anxiety in early childhood: the first at around 5 to 6 years, and another around 9 to 11 years.

Sleep disruption due to fear is generally a normal, temporary stage in children's development. When youngsters have learned to deal with the fear, they return to their previous patterns of

WATCH HOW YOU SAY IT...

A 2-year-old developed a fear of burning up at night when his parents told him they were putting a cool-mist humidifier in his bedroom. After he was able to inspect the device and its workings were explained to him, he accepted that it was not a fire but a "different kind of -fier" and his fears went away.

sleeping—good or bad. Your goal, as parent, is to bolster your child's confidence so that he can sleep in his own bed without fear of harm. The way you achieve this is different from the approach you use to establish good sleeping habits or correct poor ones. A child who is frightened needs more time and attention than one who is merely testing the limits of his parents' patience. It's important to judge where to draw the line in dealing with fears, in order to promote good sleeping habits. If your child's sleep

WHEN FEARS TAKE OVER

If your child is unusually fearful, is becoming increasingly fearful, or compulsively repeats actions, words, or rituals to ward off fears, talk to your pediatrician.

pattern was unsatisfactory before the start of the fear phase, you will have to continue working to improve it after the youngster has mastered the fear.

"ODD JOBS" TO FOSTER INDEPENDENT SLEEPING

 My 3-year-old daughter won't go to sleep unless my husband or I stay in the room. She says she's afraid now, but will sleep alone when she gets bigger. When do children grow out of this fearful phase?

Your daughter has no incentive to go to sleep on her own as long as company is available. However, it may be too much to expect her to make a major change in one go. The "odd jobs" approach may be your answer. When you have completed your bedtime routine and settled your daughter in her bed, tell her that Mommy and Daddy have things to do in another room. (Be specific: tell her the kitchen, the laundry, or any room you choose.) You will listen out for her and you'll be back in just 5 minutes. If she's upset at this plan, put a clock in her room and show her where the hands will be or what the numbers will say when it's time for you to come back. Leave the room and return in 5 minutes—no more, no less. If she cries or calls for you, answer from outside her room, but don't go back in until the 5 minutes are up.

When you go back, praise her for staying in bed, cuddle her if you like but don't let her get out of bed, then leave again on another errand, for perhaps a little longer. Make this your practice for the next several nights. Find increasingly time-consuming tasks to do in another room, but always go back briefly to your daughter's bedroom at the time you promised, even if you think she's asleep. She may resist your leaving the first few times. But as she becomes confident that you will return, she will relax, get drowsy, and eventually fall asleep.

HOW FEARS ARE MANIFESTED

Nighttime fears emerge in various ways. They are often the reason for bedtime resistance, when children dawdle, find distractions, or simply refuse to go to bed. Many children manage to put off the worst of their fears until the parents leave the bedroom or the lights are turned off. One child may come right out and say he's afraid of monsters behind the curtains, while another comes up with delaying tactics when it's time for bed. Some children frequently misbehave or throw tantrums as bedtime approaches.

AVOID TRIGGERING NIGHTTIME FEARS

- Turn off the TV, VCR, and computer games in the hour or so before bedtime. Don't allow your child to watch violent programs or play violent video or computer games at any time; monitor cartoons and news programs to shield your child from gratuitous violence and overexciting stimulation.

- Avoid roughhousing and vigorous play at bedtime.

- Read calming stories with happy endings and sing cheerful songs; avoid cliffhangers and tales that end sadly.

- Avoid talking about scary topics, including what your child finds frightening, at bedtime; hold such discussions in the light of day. Daytime is also a good time to talk about how you will respond to your child's requests at night.

- For a child who is unusually sensitive to sounds after dark, try playing a tape of soothing sounds at a very low volume while he goes to sleep.

- If your child is afraid of the dark, leave a very dim lamp or night-light switched on; turn the light off after your child has fallen asleep.

- If the sight of a picture, drape, toy, or piece of furniture always bothers your child at night, consider moving it out of the bedroom.

SOME ANXIETY IS NORMAL, SOME IS NOT

It is normal for children to feel some anxiety. Learning to cope with anxiety and not be overwhelmed by it is a healthy part of growing up. However, when anxiety begins to take over, your child needs help (also see *Panic Disorder,* p. 137). Consult your pediatrician if your child seems anxious and has:

- Difficulty falling asleep.

- Frequent waking.

- Bedtime resistance.

- Symptoms suggesting panic attacks:

  • shortness of breath.

  • faintness.

  • racing or thumping heart.

  • nausea.

  • choking sensation.

  • chest pain.

  • fear of losing control or even dying.

Others appear extremely restless once they get into bed; this may be a reaction to intrusive, troubling thoughts.

What Monsters May Stand For

While monsters aren't real, the fears they stand for are real and troubling to youngsters. For example, a child who is anxious about staying dry at night may confront her fears of bed-wetting in the form of a scary beast that comes out after dark. One who is worried about harnessing feelings of anger and jealousy may find himself under nightly attack by hostile creatures. Fantasies of aggression, which are a normal stage of development, may be particularly distressing after a child sees similar impulses acted out on

OVERCOMING FEARS IN A FIVE-YEAR-OLD

? *My 5-year-old doesn't go to bed easily. He has undergone two major changes in the last year: (1) His parents divorced; and (2) he got his own room and bed. I have tried various ways to make his room and bed special, and we follow a nightly routine. However, he worries and frets each evening as bedtime approaches, and wants to sleep with me or his big brother. I don't know if it's better to be firm and insist that he sleep alone, or allow more time for him to develop a sense of security by letting him sleep in my bed.*

It's understandable that your son would seek a comforting presence at night; however, child therapists warn that a youngster who routinely shares a bed with the parent of the opposite sex may become overstimulated and risk developing emotional problems.

Your best solution may be a compromise. Enlist your older son's support in helping the younger one become more independent. Move the 5-year-old's bed into his brother's room and have the boys share for a few months. This will let each boy have his own bed, but the younger one won't feel lonely and isolated. In the meantime, work on helping him to see a room of his own as a goal to reach for. If difficulties persist, talk to your pediatrician, who may refer your son to a counselor with experience in helping children through similar difficulties.

television or in a movie. The children themselves don't know what the monsters symbolize. For parents, who may feel perplexed about dealing with a fearful child, the best approach is to acknowledge the fears and explain that the monsters aren't real. What helps children overcome their fears is reassurance that

Joshua, almost 4, was a smart, good-natured boy who had no problems with sleeping or behavior and loved going to preschool. He welcomed the idea of having a little sister, was aware of the basic facts of pregnancy and birth, and helped his parents get a room ready for the baby's arrival.

After the first few days of adjustment, Joshua's parents wondered if they now had two babies. Joshua became tearful and whiny, demanded to sleep in the crib he'd abandoned two years before, wet his bed, and woke in the middle of the night complaining of monsters in his bedroom. For the first time, he even resisted going to school, which he had previously looked forward to.

Trusting their pediatrician's assurance that this return to babyhood was a passing phase, his parents bolstered Joshua's identity as the big boy of the family by making special time for him alone and reading stories that let him understand he wasn't the first child to feel shunted aside by a baby. They protected his mattress with a plastic sheet in case of nighttime accidents and let him choose a new night-light. Joshua's father stayed seated by his bed for a few minutes after the last bedtime story while Joshua drifted into a sleepy state. And to make sure that the monsters didn't sneak in after Daddy left, the family dog was allowed to sleep in Joshua's bedroom. In less than a month, the monsters and other troubles had vanished, and Joshua celebrated his fourth birthday with a new maturity.

Mommy and Daddy—or whoever the trusted caregiver may be—are there to protect and comfort them.

Children may not understand the urges underlying their fears, but they are aware of the disturbing feelings such urges produce. To explain away those feelings, the imagination comes up with the all-purpose scapegoat: monsters or their close relatives. Fears usually lie dormant during the daytime, when children are on the

NIGHT FEARS AND NERVOUS HABITS

? *My 7-year-old son wakes up several times every night frightened by noises. If I also have heard something, I try to explain it to him, but increasingly, there are noises that only he can hear. He gets obsessed with the noises, usually imagining that there's an intruder in the house. The only way to get him to stay in bed is to threaten punishment, but I don't like to do this. I am concerned with what causes his behavior and how to help him conquer his fears. He doesn't like to be separated from me and has other fears that adults consider irrational. Recently, he has developed several nervous habits (twitches and so on) that he can't seem to control.*

Contact your pediatrician, who will evaluate the situation and may recommend an examination by another specialist.

go, too busy to dwell on problems. However, as youngsters become sleepy and their ability to control their emotions ebbs away, fantasies flourish. At bedtime, children have to let go of the very limited control they exercise over their environment. Thus,

OTHERS HAVE FEARS, TOO

Many children are comforted by knowing that others have fears and anxieties just like theirs. Fears, nightmares, dreams, and sleep are sensitively handled in stories such as *In the Night Kitchen* and *Where the Wild Things Are* by Maurice Sendak, *There's a Nightmare in My Closet* by Mercer Mayer, and *Ben's Dream* by Chris Van Allsburg, as well as many others. Take care, however, that the stories themselves are not frightening to your child.

Real Fears

? *My 9-year-old never had a problem sleeping until a month ago, when there was a robbery at the house next door. He used to fall asleep by 9:00 P.M.; now he is frightened by every little noise and can't get to sleep until at least 10:30. Calming music hasn't worked and I don't want to try medications.*

Nighttime fears are common and reach their second and final major peak between ages 9 and 11 years. Most school-age youngsters' fears are very real to them even if groundless. In your son's case, however, his fear is understandable because—like fears of school violence—it stems from an actual event, even though it didn't involve him directly.

In addition to reassuring your child, you will need to address and master any fears of your own. One way to start is by reviewing home safety procedures with your son, including fire escape routes and how to make an emergency call. If you have an alarm system, let him read the instruction manual and practice switching the system on and off. Put him in charge of activating it at certain times. If your son is concerned about his personal safety, a martial arts course could help him develop more self-confidence. The fear triggered by this traumatic event will probably fade away after several months. If it becomes more intense, talk to your pediatrician, who will evaluate your son and may advise counseling.

nighttime emotions may overwhelm daytime logic, and the youngsters are less able to avoid troublesome thoughts. Children tend to feel and act younger than their years in this state, which psychologists call "regression." Consequently, they may need a different kind of reassurance than during the day. At times, you

A child may develop extreme nighttime fears with attacks of hysterical panic that disrupt family life. Such fears usually reflect an underlying emotional difficulty, deeper and more complicated than normal fears. In this case, your child's pediatrician should be made aware and, if he or she thinks it advisable, will provide a referral to another specialist with experience in treating childhood emotional difficulties. If the child's fears are centered on his bedroom, a form of desensitization treatment may be necessary. Parents and child together should spend increasing amounts of time in the room during the day, playing games, doing puzzles, rearranging the furniture, and finding other ways to feel at ease in the surroundings—perhaps even acting out part of the nighttime routine. Eventually, with counseling, the child will agree to sleep in his own room, possibly on his own initiative. The treatment process cannot be hurried. It demands plenty of patience and the parents must take an active part in it.

may feel you're dealing with another child at night—one who acts a year or two younger than her independent daylight self.

Managing monsters takes a two-pronged approach involving a confident, open attitude to problems during the daytime, and calm reassurance at night. Children model their coping style on their parents' behavior. If you appear calm and confident, your child will try to copy you.

FEARS IN SCHOOL-AGE CHILDREN

In young children, normal nighttime fears arise out of the child's internal struggles to come to terms with the world. By contrast, older children may be aware of many more external factors, such as overhearing parents arguing, media reports of shootings and other violence in school, or bullying at school. News programs on radio and TV, movies, and violent computer games can stimulate frightening images. Children who feel frustrated because of their inability to deal with matters beyond their control may suffer depression mixed in with stress and fearfulness.

A school-age child who is losing sleep because of nighttime fears should be evaluated by a pediatrician. Counseling may be advised to help the family sort out its problems.

Managing Monsters

The best way to deal with the monsters and demons that come out at night is to reassure your child that she is safe in her own home, and Mommy and Daddy are looking after her. Variations on this approach depend on the individual child's personality. For some children, challenging the monsters on their own turf—shining a light in the closet, as Matthew's mother did, or sweeping under the bed—is only an acknowledgment that the monsters are real and thus to be feared. The child may also seize the opportunity to stretch out bedtime with challenging questions, such as: "How do you know the monsters didn't hide when they heard you coming?" Other children respond favorably to such monster-eradication methods.

It's not necessary to get to the bottom of the fears by questioning your child at bedtime; it may be better to save discussions for the bright light of day. If your child is upset, sit in a chair beside his bed, rub his back if it calms him, and reply to his questions without speaking any more than you have to. Let him know you understand how he feels, but confidently and supportively reassure him. When he is calm, sleepy, but still awake, quietly leave the room, leaving the door open so that the child does not feel cut off and you can check on him, if necessary, without disturbing him. Once he's asleep, shut the door as recommended for fire safety by the American Academy of Pediatrics (see p. 79).

Occasionally, your child is unusually upset and renews his frightened behavior whenever you try to leave the room. On these nights, you may find it best to sit in a chair next to his bed or even lie on the floor, if that's more comfortable. Try not to use this approach several nights in a row or you may find yourself with a

Seeking Comfort from the Familiar

? *We have a daughter, 7, and a son, 3. Both slept fine and in their own beds until we moved to a new house. Now they want to sleep in the same bedroom, even though they have their own rooms. When we insist that they sleep apart, my son crawls into bed with my husband and me after we're asleep. Should I be concerned that they refuse to sleep in their own rooms?*

Children frequently feel a little shaken and insecure on moving to a new house, no matter how much they looked forward to the change. Let your children have separate beds in the same room if they want to. They're not necessarily rejecting the new bedrooms you have provided. They are simply seeking comfort from something familiar: namely, each other. Give them time to get used to their new surroundings and try not to impose more changes than they can handle at one time. In a few months, they'll probably be ready for rooms of their own.

whole new set of difficulties. Your child may quickly come to depend on your presence to fall asleep, whereas your goal is to help him learn to get to sleep on his own. There are ways to deal with the problem and yet, at the same time, avoid fostering dependence. One is to sit in your child's room several nights in a row. Each night, move your chair a little farther away from your child's bed until you are sitting outside the room, in the passageway, still within your child's earshot and prepared to respond to his cries, if need be. Finally, when he is used to seeing you go out of the room to get to the chair, you will no longer have to keep sitting in the chair to reassure him. This method of gradual distancing may take a week or two to complete.

When a young child is frightened, you may have to relax the

rule about picking her up. Try to comfort her in her crib or bed, but be prepared to give her a cuddle, if that's what it takes. However, keep the lights (except a night-light) off, stay in her room, and avoid giving in to her requests to sleep in your bed or to join other family members who are still up. If you bring your child to your room or let her stay up, you're putting off the moment of reckoning. The aim in calming your child's fears is to reassure her that her own bed is the most appropriate and comfortable place for her to sleep. Letting her sleep away from her bed not only rewards her for staying awake but may also increase the fear that her bedroom is not a safe place.

DELIVER US FROM EAGLES...

For many families, prayers are part of the going-to-bed routine. However, the images conjured up by certain prayers may be troubling to imaginative young children, for whom notions of sleep and death tend to overlap. Teach simple prayers with words that comfort and that your child can easily understand.

A child who is afraid of sleeping in a room alone may be happier sharing with a sister or brother, if there's room for two beds. The advantages of sharing with a confident, protective older sibling are obvious; however, toddlers and preschoolers may also lose their nighttime fears when the baby of the family graduates from a bassinet in the parents' room to a crib in the older child's room.

SLEEP AND DEATH

The death of someone close to the child or of a pet may release a flood of anxiety and nighttime fears. Children's concerns are frequently centered on the notion of falling asleep and never waking again. Such fears are fed when adults use euphemisms that talk about sleep instead of death: "We had to put kitty to sleep," or

ANXIETY AND MOURNING

 I have a 10-year-old who lost his father last year. Since then he seems to be unable to sleep by himself in his own bed.

Explain to your son that you understand his anxiety, but that both of you must get proper rest in your own beds. Ask your pediatrician about how to help children after bereavement. Some families find it helpful to receive counseling together rather than individually.

"Granddad went to sleep and he won't wake up anymore."

The child's sense of loss may not be deep if the person who has died was only occasionally present in his life. However, grieving for someone closer may involve complicated feelings of sadness, anger, and fear. Children are sometimes engulfed by grief they cannot express when their usual caregivers leave or are replaced.

In explaining death to a child it's best to use the correct words and provide the simple, straightforward facts, keeping concepts of sleep and death in their proper places: "Grandpa's heart stopped working because he was old and very ill." A similar approach should be used to explain the departure of a familiar childcare helper: "Peggy can't help us any longer because she has gone to live too far away, so now we're lucky to have Betty to help look after you." Most important in both situations is the reassurance that "Mommy and Daddy are here to look after you."

SETTING LIMITS

Parents become highly attuned to their children's behavior. However, at times it can be difficult to tell whether your child is genuinely frightened or is just putting on a convincing show. After several nights of receiving extra attention in response to crying, a child may decide to extend the performance in a bid to

Abuse Makes a Child Fearful

An unusual fear of going to bed may be a sign that a child is being subjected to physical or sexual abuse, particularly in the preschool years. Your child may be too young or too frightened to tell you the cause of his fears, or the predator may have threatened harm if the child tells. If you suspect abuse, or have concerns about the influence of children or adults with whom your child has been spending time, whether at home or away, consult your pediatrician. He or she will examine your child for signs of abuse and may be able to draw out information that your child is afraid to talk about with those closer to him. If abuse has occurred, your pediatrician will suggest a course of action to lessen the impact and may recommend counseling for your child and the whole family.

keep the attention coming. This is where parents have to be prepared to set limits. Stay in your child's room while calming him. Give his worries a fair hearing, but keep your responses brief and to the point: "You're safe in your bed. I'm looking after you." Avoid becoming involved in discussions that may feed the fears and prolong the wakefulness.

CHAPTER 8

Nightmares, Sleep Terrors, and Partial Arousals

Alex, age 2, whimpered as he woke up from a nap: "See elephant. Elephant have sharp teeth. It chase me. It bite my pajamas!" The toddler's face crumpled and he curled against his mother as if to hide from the angry animal.

"The elephant can't get you. It wasn't a real, live elephant. You just had a scary dream. Real elephants are friendly and gentle. One day soon we'll go see one at the zoo."

Thanks to EEG studies of brain waves, we know that REM, or dreaming, sleep takes up a good part of an infant's sleep time. In fact, during the first 3 months, babies begin

> *In contrast to some other sleep disturbances, dreams and nightmares are normal—part of our mind's mechanism for working out emotional conflicts that arise in the waking hours.*

each period of sleep with an active REM phase (see Chapter 1). However, we have no way of telling whether it's dreaming that prompts the little smiles, sighs, and frowns we see in sleeping babies. What we do know is that toddlers begin to report dreams and nightmares as soon as they can say enough words to do so. For many, this occurs quite early in the second year.

Nightmares are certainly upsetting. A child awakens crying and fearful, needing comfort and reassurance. Very young children may need to be told repeatedly that monsters aren't "real, live ones," so the monsters can't hurt them, and Mommy and Daddy will keep them safe.

BEDTIME FEARS FOLLOWING NIGHTMARES

 My 4½-year-old daughter has frequent nightmares and now is afraid to go to bed.

Nightmares are common in young children and usually reflect an emotionally upsetting situation, which is part of normal development. Even though your daughter, at age 4½, knows that what she sees in a dream is not real, her nightmares are very frightening. A child who has become apprehensive about having more bad dreams needs a lot of reassurance and support.

To help her relax at bedtime, sit in her room for a few nights while she goes to sleep. Once she is used to becoming drowsy in your presence, you can try the "odd job" method (see p. 130) to foster independence. Using this approach, find increasingly time-consuming jobs to do away from your child's room, but always return at the promised time. Leave a night-light on and the door ajar so your daughter can orient herself.

Before you go to bed, shut the doors to all sleeping rooms. The American Academy of Pediatrics recommends that doors to sleeping rooms be kept shut at night as a fire safety measure.

When your child's sleep is broken by a nightmare, give her physical comfort and soothing words. If she wants to talk about the frightening images, let her do so and reassure her that they can't hurt her. Otherwise, save discussions about scary images for the daylight hours. You may occasionally need to sit down next to her while she becomes drowsy. However, avoid making a habit of it because, if prolonged, it may bring on further disruption of sleep when you leave the bedroom.

HECK FOR CAUSES OTHER THAN NIGHTMARE

A child may awaken crying and fretful for reasons other than nightmares. Check for fever and symptoms suggesting an ear infection, stomach upset (gastroenteritis), or another illness that could be making your child unhappy. Your child may have an arm or leg caught in the crib bars, or may be in pain because a hair is twisted around a finger or toe (also see p. 83). You may have to retrieve a favorite transitional object—a toy, a pacifier, or a blanket—and put it back where your child can feel it for comfort.

Almost everybody has a dream vivid and scary enough to count as a nightmare from time to time. Both children and adults often have nightmares during illness, especially if fever is present and treatment with medication is required.

REAMS ARE REAL EVEN IF MONSTERS AREN'T

A child under age 2 has difficulty grasping the difference between dreams and real life, as Alex did with his elephant. Comfort and cuddle a child who wakes crying from a scary dream, just as you would after any other frightening experience.

WHY CHILDREN HAVE NIGHTMARES. What a child dreams about is influenced by three factors: his level of emotional and physical development; the emotional conflicts the child is dealing with at his particular developmental stage; and daytime events that the child finds unusually threatening. Experts stress that nightmares are normal and must be kept in perspective. One authority on children's sleep sums up nightmares as follows:

Although most nightmares do reflect ongoing emotional conflicts, in most cases neither the nightmares nor the conflicts are 'abnormal.' Rather, the normal emotional struggles associated with growing up are at times significant enough to lead to occasional nightmares.

EARLY NIGHTMARES. The concerns that resurface as nightmares are generally the same ones that trigger nighttime fears and bedtime resistance (also see Chapter 7). The earliest such concern is recurrent separation anxiety (see pp. 19 and 84), which may be triggered by any number of scary notions. Typically, worries can include fear of getting lost or being left at childcare, the arrival of a new baby, or a parent's temporary absence on a business trip. A slightly older child in the midst of toilet training may be torn

Toilet Training Shouldn't Be a Nightmare

If frequent nightmares are disturbing your toddler during toilet training, take the pressure off. Encourage your youngster to relax with "messy" play such as finger paints, water, and play dough.

between the desire to please his parents and an inability to resist soiling. On the one hand, he fears a lack of control; on the other, he wants to assert his independence. Dreams at this age typically reflect the anxiety such stress produces, and threatening or humiliating monsters are part of the regular cast of characters.

A child between ages 3 and 6 years has to find ways to resolve many impulses involving aggression and sexuality. For example, a youngster feeling naturally jealous of an addition to the family may struggle with an urge to harm the new arrival. At this age, too, she may be pleased but troubled by the pleasurable feelings she gets from touching her genitals. These conflicting feelings are frightening because the child worries that if her parents know about them, they will be angry and punish her. The parents' role here is to let the child know that it's normal to have both pleasurable and negative feelings, but that there are limits to how we act on them. You need to help your child learn to control her impulses and behave in a socially acceptable manner. A toddler's gentle patting of the new baby may turn into punching, or she may come right out and say, "I hate that baby!" In this case, help her to understand that you love her and know how she feels. At the same time, show her that you love the baby as well, and will not tolerate actions that could harm him.

Stories are a wonderful way to get the message across, partly because reading a story has the added bonus of giving your youngster one-on-one parent time that a new baby isn't old enough to share. Check your local bookstore and library for books that deal with the issues in language appropriate to your child's age level. Praise your child for being a big girl and enlist her help with babycare tasks. Perhaps encourage her to care for a pet or a favorite toy as you look after the baby.

At the same time, you must help your child understand the difference between unacceptable behavior and truly wrongful acts, and she must be able to trust your example. A child who is

:XUAL ANXIETY MAY CAUSE NIGHTMARES IN PRESCHOOLERS

Anxiety stemming from sexual stimulation can cause nightmares in preschoolers. A child may be trying to sort out conflicting feelings caused by sexually stimulating play with a friend or sibling. Or he may be confused and upset by sounds overheard from his parents' bedroom. Little girls of this age tend to be possessive toward their fathers and feel rivalry toward their mothers, whereas boys yearn for their mothers and want to replace their fathers, even perhaps to the extent of pushing and kicking them out of bed.

Psychologists warn that anxieties about sexual issues may be intensified when children are regularly allowed to sleep in the parents' bed. A child who is having nightmares and sleep disturbances should be helped to calm down, then led back to his own bed. Although he may protest at first, eventually he will be happier—and the whole family will sleep better—if the parents set limits and stick to them.

Dealing with Nightmares

Sleep researchers have developed methods that may help children to reprogram scary dreams. Children who had frequent nightmares were instructed by sleep researchers to close their eyes while awake and remember their nightmares, and to consciously change the course of the nightmare from a frightening ending to a happy one. After only a few sessions of reprogramming, the children's nightmares began to follow the pleasant scenarios they had rehearsed during the daytime sessions. This technique may be worth trying for a child who often has upsetting dreams.

exposed to loud arguments and violent speech or conduct in the family home will have trouble with her own behavior if she senses that her parents lack self-control. In other words, they fail to practice what they preach.

SCHOOL-AGE NIGHTMARES. Nightmares occur somewhat less frequently after age 6 and before about 11, when most children have overcome their early conflicts and have yet to plunge into the turmoil of puberty. For the most part, youngsters of school age are adept at managing new challenges as they come along. However, troubling situations at school can emerge as nightmares. Bullying, poor communication with teachers, cliquishness, and teasing provoked by lack of athletic or social skills may recur in the form of nightmares or night waking, with anxiety or depression. If your child is sleeping either much less or much more than usual, often complains of vague symptoms such as headaches or stomachaches, finds excuses not to go to school, or expresses feelings of worthlessness, he may need help in dealing with school problems. Consult with teachers to identify specific difficulties and arrange an appointment with your pediatrician, who will examine your child and may refer him to an experienced counselor.

ADOLESCENCE. Disturbing dreams may be more frequent with the onrush of anxieties and insecurities at adolescence. If your teenager tells you she's having nightmares, there may be something else she wants to talk about (also see Chapter 11). Try to pick up on the cues she drops but don't probe so deeply that you risk cutting off communications.

WHEN TO SEEK HELP. An occasional bad dream is nothing to worry about. However, if a child frequently wakes at night with nightmares or at other times seems unduly emotional—tearful, timid, clingy, bad-tempered, impulsive, hard to control—talk to your pediatrician. The results of an examination may suggest the need for counseling or another treatment. If a young child is having nightmares because there is conflict between the parents, counseling for the whole family may be advised.

MIT YOUR CHILD'S EXPOSURE TO SCARY IMAGES

Monitor the videos, movies, and TV programs your child watches, including news broadcasts. Although your child may "enjoy" such shows in the daytime, the images can bring on anxiety and nightmares later on, when he has time to reflect on them.

PARTIAL AROUSALS: SLEEPWALKING, SLEEPTALKING, SLEEP TERRORS

Children's sleep is punctuated by episodes of partial arousal. For infants and young children, stage IV non-REM sleep is even more intense than it is for older children and adults. The spell of sleep is not fully broken by the internal arousal switches that signal the end of the first two sleep cycles of the night. In almost all cases, partial arousals are of no consequence. However, the form they take and their significance, if any, vary according to the child's age, health, and development.

A tendency to partial arousals with sleep terrors or sleepwalking may run in the family. When there is a family history, a child under age 6 with partial arousals is said to have a biological or genetic predisposition; in a child older than 6, stress in the

After children fall asleep, they rapidly pass into stage IV non-REM sleep, the deepest form of non-dreaming sleep (also see p. 9). This phase, called the first sleep cycle, lasts from 60 to 90 minutes. The next cycle involves lighter sleep and possibly a brief arousal, then terminates with a rapid return to Stage IV non-REM. Once these two initial cycles are over, youngsters spend the rest of the night switching back and forth between lighter stages of non-REM sleep and REM (active dreaming) periods, which tend to become longer with more intense dreaming toward morning.

Although children in non-REM sleep may appear to be battling monsters or trying to escape from tight situations, they are not having dreams they will remember. Sleep experts believe that during non-REM sleep and in the transition from one sleep cycle to another, the body's deep-sleep and waking systems are both active at the same time. In this state, sleepers are said to be in a state of partial arousal. Children may talk, move, and walk at these times. They may sit up, look around, and appear frightened and upset, but they do not communicate in any meaningful way. Although a child may look as if he's awake, he is still sleeping; he cannot perform actions that involve higher brain functions, such as reading or working on a puzzle. A child in this state does not record events in his memory. By contrast, during REM sleep, the body is virtually paralyzed—the dreamer cannot sit up, move, walk, or talk—but the mind is actively involved in dreaming. The dreams we remember are those that occur during this state. Perhaps the near-paralysis is a safety device: nature's way of making sure we don't injure ourselves while acting out or trying to escape from alarming images.

family or the child's environment may trigger an emotional predisposition. Sleep experts affirm that sleep terrors, sleepwalking, and other forms of episodic partial arousal in children up to age

5 or 6 are almost never signs that something is seriously amiss. However, when such episodes appear for the first time in an older child or occur with unusual intensity, they may be tied to underlying emotional issues and treatment may be required.

SLEEP TERRORS. Sleep terrors (also called night terrors) are seen most often in preschoolers and early school-age children—ages 2 to 6. They may occur in toddlers, but if an episode occurs before age 1 year, the baby should be examined by a pediatrician.

During a sleep terror, the child cries or screams and thrashes around the bed. Her eyes are usually wide open and her facial expression is strange. One reason that parents find such partial arousals upsetting is that their child looks and acts so differently from her usual self. Her heart is racing and she may be drenched

RY AN EARLIER BEDTIME

Some children have sleep terrors when they are overtired. Putting the child to bed half an hour earlier may prevent sleep terrors in such cases.

in sweat. Her movements may be so odd and forceful that the parents call their pediatrician to report an epileptic seizure. The parents' natural urge is to pick the child up and wake her out of what seems to be a bad dream. However, a child in the midst of a sleep terror does not calm down when her parents intervene. Even though she may have called out their names, she probably will not respond to their touch and will become even more agitated when they try to rouse her.

Sleep terrors are much worse for the parents than for the child. Even though a child may scream in apparent fear or call out, "No, no!" or "I can't!" she may not be having a nightmare and will certainly remember nothing on waking. Episodes of sleep terrors last, on average, between 5 and 30 minutes and may recur several times a night. After an episode is over, the child will probably calm down—if she has awoken—and fall back to sleep.

If you are able to awaken your child from a sleep terror, your own nervousness may upset her and prevent her from settling back to sleep. Questioned closely, she may make up a nightmarish

---

SLEEP TERRORS IN A TODDLER

? *About once a week, my toddler screams in the middle of the night. What I don't understand is that he's asleep during the screaming and it takes us several minutes to wake him. After we do so, it takes him half an hour to calm down. Why is he doing this? Is something wrong?*

It sounds as if your toddler is experiencing sleep terrors. Talk to your pediatrician who will examine your child and advise you on the best course to follow. Sleep terrors, while frightening for parents, are unusual but not abnormal; in time, children outgrow them. Like sleepwalking, sleep terrors occur during partial arousals from the deepest phase of non-REM sleep. Episodes may occur as often as twice a week; they usually last for 5 to 10 minutes but some may go on for half an hour. If attacks occur more often than twice a week and last longer than 30 minutes, ask your pediatrician for an evaluation.

During sleep terrors (in contrast to nightmares), your child is not awake and, despite the screams, is not having a bad dream—at least, not one that he will remember. It's hard to wake a child during an episode of sleep terrors. He may only become more agitated and try to push you away.

Surprisingly, a youngster does not remember sleep terrors, even right after being awakened. Although you naturally want to comfort your child, it's best not to wake him up. Instead, let the episode run its course. Afterward, your child will settle back to sleep.

dream to satisfy you and end up by believing it herself. Finally, when a somewhat older child awakens suddenly with a pounding heart and other sensations she associates with fear, she may falsely "remember" a dream to explain the feelings to herself. Try to stay calm and don't try to awaken your child in the grip of sleep terrors. Simply allow the episode to run its course.

DEALING WITH SLEEP TERRORS

The best way to deal with sleep terrors:

- Gently hug or stroke your child, if she will tolerate the contact.

- Don't shake the child, question her, or try to offer comfort except for a cuddle and a whispered, "I'm here."

- Keep the lights dim and speak quietly.

- Wait out the episode and stay with your child until she has calmed down and is settling for sleep.

- Remove hazardous or unstable objects to prevent injury in case your child walks during a terror; check the rest of your home for safety (for additional tips, see p. 157).

- Some children have sleep terrors when they are overtired. Putting your child to bed about half an hour earlier may help prevent sleep terrors.

Some children have sleep terrors repeatedly, whereas others have only a single episode. Even recurrent sleep terrors disappear naturally, without treatment, as the child matures. In rare cases, a child older than about 5 who has very frequent sleep terrors may develop a fear of going to sleep. To prevent the onset of a more severe behavioral problem in such a child, your pediatrician may prescribe a sedative medication to calm the child before bedtime. The medication is taken in a very low dose, and treatment is usually required for no longer than a month.

Nightmare vs. Sleep Terror

	Nightmare	Sleep Terror
What is it?	A frightening dream occurring during REM sleep	Partial arousal from very deep, non-REM (nondreaming) sleep
How do you know it's happening?	Afterward, your child wakes up and tells you	During a sleep terror your child screams and moves about
When does it happen?	In the latter part of the night, when dreams are most intense	Usually between 1 and 4 hours after falling asleep
Child's appearance and behavior	Crying and fearful	Screaming, talking, thrashing about; sweating, heart racing; frightened
Awareness	On waking, child is aware of surroundings and reassured by parent's presence	Child does not fully awaken; may become more agitated if parents try to rouse him
Return to sleep	May have trouble falling asleep because of fear of nightmare images	Usually calms down and settles back to sleep without becoming fully awake
Memory	Remembers dream and may relate it	Has no memory of behavior or of a dream

Adapted from *Solve Your Child's Sleep Problems,* by Richard Ferber, M.D.

Pediatricians offer two general rules for handling children with sleep terrors and nightmares:

- Be watchful but don't try to awaken a child during a sleep terror.
- Comfort and support a child with a nightmare.

SLEEPWALKING. Sleepwalking, like sleep terrors and sleeptalking, occurs when a child wakes incompletely out of non-dreaming sleep. About 15 out of every 100 children between ages 6 and 16 walk in their sleep from time to time. It can be alarming for parents to see their child wandering about, apparently awake but unresponsive. However, for children who begin sleepwalking before age 10 and stop by about 15, sleepwalking is not associated with problems of behavior or personality. Although sleepwalking is not necessarily a symptom of emotional stress, many sleepwalkers tend to make their rounds more often when they are feeling stressed, such as at school exam time.

Children usually begin their nighttime rambles within 2 to 3 hours after falling asleep. The gait may be hesitant or stumbling, and the child's walking is usually aimless, although a sleepwalker may also perform other actions such as dressing, opening doors and drawers, and raiding the refrigerator. An episode may last as long as half an hour.

There's no need to rouse a sleepwalker. In fact, if you try to do so, your child will be disoriented and, as with sleep terrors, may become distressed on waking. Better gently to guide her back to bed. She'll wake up in the morning with no memory of the event.

SLEEPTALKING. In contrast to sleepwalking and sleep terrors, so many children and adults talk, laugh, and cry out in their sleep that talking in one's sleep is not considered a sleep problem or even unusual behavior. As with sleepwalking, children do not talk during the active-dreaming REM-sleep periods but, instead, while crossing over between non-REM and REM phases. Although a sleeptalker may appear to respond to questions, he is not aware and should not be held accountable for anything he says. A sleeptalker retains no memory of the event and it is pointless to question him the next morning, even though you may be under the impression you shared a conversation with him.

TOOTH GRINDING. Many children grind their teeth with a loud, grating sound while asleep. Like other forms of partial arousal, tooth grinding, or bruxism, occurs during transitions between REM and non-REM sleep phases. It doesn't mean that your child is having a nightmare or reliving a frustrating event from the daytime. There is no connection between tooth grinding and problems of behavior or personality. In most cases it is unlikely to damage the teeth; however, if you have any concerns, check with your child's dentist and mention it at each regular dental checkup. Tooth grinding becomes less common as children grow older, but many adults continue to grind their teeth.

HEAD BANGING IN AN INFANT

 Since age 3 months, my daughter has repeatedly banged her head before falling asleep. What can I do to stop her? Simply saying "Stop!" doesn't help.

Head banging and body rocking are quite common and normal. While alarming to parents, these activities are harmless to the child and gradually stop. Children usually outgrow rocking, rolling, and head banging between 18 months and 2 years of age. If the activity continues or becomes more intense, ask your pediatrician for an evaluation.

BODY ROCKING AND HEAD BANGING

Rhythmic, repetitious activity at bedtime is a common early childhood behavior that seems to calm the child even as it mystifies the parents. It's hard to understand how a toddler could derive comfort from rocking back and forth on all fours while knocking his head—hard—into the railings of his crib, or sitting up and bumping his upper body against the headboard, or lying face down and banging his head on the mattress 60 to 80 times a minute. Nevertheless, at least 10 percent of young children soothe themselves in this way for up to half an hour and even longer while preparing for sleep, and probably twice that number also repeatedly rock, bump, or bang their heads at intervals during the day when fully awake.

You can't stop your baby from banging, but you can take steps to keep the noise at the lowest possible level. Pull the crib away from the wall and stand it on a thick rug. Pad the crib with a tight-fitting fabric that reaches all around the sides and over the top railing. Secure the padding with several ties at top and bottom to keep it from falling open and providing a foot- or handhold for your child. Trim the ties to no more than 6 inches

DOUBLE-CHECK YOUR HOME FOR SAFETY IF THERE'S A SLEEPWALKER

- Install window guards that can be opened in case of fire.

- If there is a risk that your child might try to go through a closed window, replace regular window glass with unbreakable panes.

- If your sleepwalker is an older child or adolescent, have him sleep on the lowest level of the house.

- If your children sleep in bunk beds, have your sleepwalker use the lower bunk.

- Place childproof safety gates at the top and bottom of stairs.

- Put breakable ornaments out of reach, and clear the floor of objects, including rugs, that could cause a sleepwalker to trip and fall.

- Attach a bell to the bedroom door so you can hear when the sleepwalker leaves the bedroom.

- Check the kitchen for potential problems, such as accessible knives, a stove that can easily be turned on, or counters that can be scaled; lock the kitchen door at night if necessary to protect your sleepwalking child.

To Keep Noise to a Tolerable Level:

- Pull your rocker's crib away from the wall and set it on a thick rug.

- Fit rubber carpet protectors on the crib feet to cut down on noise and make it harder for the crib to move as the child rocks.

- Try playing a metronome or music with a strong beat to regulate the child's rhythm.

- Some parents try a padded bumper securely fastened around the crib, but a really determined rocker may pull the bumper aside to get more "bang."

- For a very young infant, try stringing a baby gym across the top of the crib, hooking up an activity center, or hanging a mobile with diverting shapes and a built-in music box. (Watch your baby's reaction to gyms and mobiles; some find them frightening and cry until they are taken away. In any case, gyms, mobiles, and crib bumpers must be removed at 5 months, the age when most babies seriously try to sit, get up on all fours, or pull themselves upright on the crib bars.)

long and double-knot them. Some pediatricians suggest using a metronome or playing music with a strong beat to help regulate the rate of the banging.

These activities are slightly more common in boys than in girls, and usually appear within the first year; 6 to 9 months is the average age. In the vast majority of cases, they are not associated with developmental delays, although children who have certain types of disability, including autism, also often become absorbed in repetitive movements. If a child reached normal developmental milestones before starting the activity, parents have nothing to be concerned about—except noise and sleep disruption. And in a child with developmental delays, the primary problem is almost always recognized before the repetitive behavior emerges.

Contrary to parents' natural fears, body rocking and head banging are unlikely to cause injury. Most youngsters outgrow the habit by about 2 years, although less intense repetitive actions may sometimes be seen in older children and adolescents. Nobody knows why children shake, rattle, and roll in this way; however, researchers are working on the finding that such rhythmic activities stimulate the vestibular system of the inner ear, which regulates balance. Some children go through a limited phase of banging or rocking at about the same time they are mastering a major developmental skill, such as learning to stand up or walk on their own.

Most children appear to rock for their own comfort, but some may use the behavior as a means of getting notice. If you always go to your child's room when you hear the sound, you may be unintentionally teaching your child to bang and knock for atten-

SHAKE, RATTLE AND ROLL...

Rocking seems to be comforting for young children. Parents take advantage of it by rocking back and forth as they soothe a baby or rhythmically pushing a baby carriage to and fro to calm an infant down.

Most babies rock from time to time and about one child in five gets up on all fours to rock at least once a day. Although rocking is soothing, youngsters don't just rock while drowsy and preparing to nap. They move while fully alert and often while listening to music. About half of the daytime rockers also rock in bed before going to sleep, and a small number of them engage in more elaborate rhythmical movements, including head banging and head rolling.

Once many head bangers can pull themselves upright, they hold onto the crib rails and bang their heads there. A really committed head banger may manage to stand, rock, bang his head, suck his thumb, and cuddle his "lovey" all at the same time.

tion. Provided your child is younger than 4, is not distressed, and usually drops off to sleep after his rhythmic interlude, you can safely leave him to rock and/or roll. However, if the behavior has suddenly appeared in an older child or when conditions in the home are unusually stressful—such as during a period of illness or marital discord—talk to your pediatrician, who may want to examine the child and recommend counseling or other treatment.

Aside from a few little bumps and bruises, bangers and rockers rarely hurt themselves. However, for a youngster with developmental disabilities, your pediatrician may prescribe a short-term medication to calm the child and recommend a helmet to prevent head injury. The helmet may have to be worn both day and night.

CHAPTER 9

Twins and More

Multiple births, once very rare, have become almost an everyday occurrence with recent advances in assisted reproduction. The rate of identical twinning—two children developed from a single egg—has stayed the same, but the frequency of fraternal (multiple-egg) twins and triplets is soaring, thanks to treatments based on the harvesting and fertilization of several eggs at a time. The greater the number of babies born from a single pregnancy, the greater the likelihood that they will be premature and smaller than babies born at term. For that reason, many of the sleep patterns and disruptions seen in twins and multiples are the same as those seen in premature and low-birth-weight infants (also see p. 38).

Sleep problems related specifically to multiple births seldom persist after the first year of your babies' lives. After that, the situation is similar to having children who are just very close in age.

When your expected baby turns out to be two babies, or three—or more—the potential for sleep problems is doubled or tripled and so is the work involved in dealing with them. But, luckily, you can also have twice as much pleasure and sense of accomplishment when problems are under control.

No matter how self-reliant you were before your babies arrived on the scene, this is one time when it's truly difficult to go it alone. Don't be afraid to ask for help. Your family and friends will probably be glad to lend a hand.

Where Do We Start?

The first goal after you bring your twins or "multiplets" home is to get them on to the same schedule for feeding, playing, bathing and dressing, and—above all—sleeping. If you don't tackle this problem from the start, you'll soon be overwhelmed by the babies' demands, your fatigue, and the sheer impossibility of being in several places at once. No matter how well organized you may be, you're bound to need help—at least to start with—in feeding, bathing, dressing, diapering, and playing with two or more little people at once, especially if you already have other children at home.

If professional help is beyond your budget, a high school or college student may welcome the chance to earn some pocket money as a part-time helper. Friends and relatives are often pleased to help out. Several parents of multiple infants have been kept afloat in the early months by rosters of volunteer helpers from their churches, temples, and local service organizations. When someone offers assistance, don't be bashful; ask "When can you come?" Keep a calendar for signing up helpers and call to confirm scheduled appointments, otherwise you may find yourself with more help than you need one day and all on your own the next. Eventually, as the babies settle into a regular routine and learn to self-soothe, fewer extra hands will be needed.

Who's on First?

It's well recognized that multiples, especially identical twins, share a special bond, with forms of communication and possibly even a sense of identity that are different from those in single offspring. Although closeness is a characteristic to be treasured, it's important that parents train themselves from the start to regard their twins or multiples as individuals. One way to do this is by making a point of referring to the children by name or as "the children," "the girls," or "the boys"—but never as "the twins." The family budget will dictate how the children are to be dressed. To foster their individual identities, however, it's probably a good idea to

One mother was concerned about promoting the individual identities of her twin daughters. She took pains, for example, never to dress the identical girls in similar outfits. When they received matching clothing as gifts, she alternately gave both outfits to one child or the other, and the girls thus took turns in getting a set and a spare. She cut their hair differently and, when they were past the toddler stage, encouraged separate friendships and play dates. Going to bed alone and learning self-soothing skills alone were part of the individualized approach. At age 5, the girls enjoyed their independence in most aspects, but begged and pleaded until their parents agreed to put their twin beds in a single room.

aim for different outfits or, at least, for contrasting colors when they wear similar outfits.

Parents of identical twins, in particular, sometimes find that their children take on complementary roles—in a sense, playing the two halves of a coin and avoiding competition with each other. For example, one girl may look after the literary side of schoolwork—emphasizing reading and writing—for both her sister and herself, while the other takes care of science and mathematics. Schools usually assign twins and multiples to different classes to encourage individual development. Separating the children early in their school career can help to ensure that each child develops his or her interests more evenly over the range of subjects.

AFTER YOU...

A common fear of parents of twin infants is that when one child starts crying, the other will follow suit. There's a tendency, therefore, to rush into the bedroom at the first whimper and placate baby A with a picking-up or a feeding in order to keep her quiet

Two by Two

? *Twins are due 3 months from now and I'm already losing sleep worrying about how I'm going to juggle two babies when they wake up for nighttime feedings. Do I feed one, then the other? What happens if they both cry at the same time?*

Now is a good time to contact your pediatrician, who will be able to reassure you with some useful advice about night feedings in newborn twins. Your pediatrician may also suggest that you get in touch with a lactation consultant—a specially trained nurse or other health professional—who is experienced in helping mothers of multiple births prepare for breastfeeding. To make it easier, a mother is sometimes advised to express breastmilk and have her partner bottle-feed one baby while she breast-feeds the other. In this way, the babies take turns at the breast and Dad has an opportunity to share in nighttime care. Be prepared, but take the lead from your babies and don't anticipate problems. When the time comes, you'll manage beautifully.

and thus avoid waking baby B. The risk is that by responding too quickly, you may foster a sleep/wake problem if one infant tends to cry more than the other. If you pick her up to soothe her, or offer an unscheduled and unnecessary feeding, she may develop a habit of waking at the same time every night.

Surprisingly, many twins and multiples don't wake each other, at least in the first year or so. Most of the time, one baby will sleep through the other's crying—perhaps only to wake up for his turn as soon as the first has settled down. When you have more than two babies, however, the chances of at least two waking up at the same time are much greater. Once the night feeding phase is over, nighttime wakings in multiples are best handled as recommended for single children (see p. 39).

If one or more babies need a clean diaper, attend to the change with the least possible disturbance. Keep the room dim; speak softly and only as much as you have to; change the diaper in the crib if you can, and put the baby right back to bed. When everybody's needs have been attended to, quickly leave the room.

If a baby keeps on crying longer than a few minutes after you leave (5 to 10 minutes is a general guideline, but with multiple babies you may want to wait a shorter time if you are concerned about disturbing the others), go back into the room without turning on the light, pat your crying baby or rub him gently and quietly tell him it's time to sleep, then leave again. Repeat your visits as necessary, but be firm: No picking up. (Also see Chapter 5, "Controversies and Strategies.")

When more than one baby is awake and crying, it may be too much for one person to handle. Occasionally, parents are in a position to employ caregivers for nighttime care. Other lucky families have a grandparent or other relative who has the time and inclination to lend a hand. In most families, however, parents eventually have to find the best way to manage on their own. This is no time for one parent to hold back with "It's your turn, I went last time." Both have to pitch in. This exhausting phase will pass, and a cooperative attitude will make it much easier.

ALL TOGETHER NOW…OR SEPARATE BUT EQUAL?

One early question you'll have to address is whether your twins or multiples will have separate bedrooms (space in your home permitting) or share a room. There are two schools of thought on this issue. Parents firmly on the side of separate rooms prefer that their multiples get used to seeing themselves as individuals right from the start. Such parents generally try to maintain a "separate but equal" policy in all aspects of their children's care.

The difficulty with this method is that even though the children are on the same schedule, you may have to stagger bedtimes somewhat. One solution is to alternate the rooms in which the

Two in a Bed

? *I have just found out that the baby we planned is going to be twins. The only room we can set aside is quite small and I don't see how we could fit two cribs in it. Would it be all right to have our babies share a crib?*

In general, it is recommended for safety that each child have an individual bassinet, crib, or bed. However, if your twins are born at term, are similar in size, and have no health problems, no harm would be done if they slept at opposite ends of the same crib for the first several weeks. Sleeping bag-pajamas would be preferable to covers for keeping the babies warm. Of course, if either child should have a health problem—a cold, for example—or require special care such as the use of a respiratory monitor, bed sharing would be out of the question. Once your babies start to become mobile, rolling over or raising themselves up on their forearms, they should be moved to separate cribs.

Perhaps, in the time before your twins are born, you may be able to reconfigure the space you've set aside. For example, it may be possible to gain space by using part of a hallway or a closet with the door removed. If the cribs are placed side by side or end to end where your babies can see each other, they will thrive on each other's company on waking and going to sleep.

nighttime routine takes place. If both parents are always available at bedtime, they may split the work to give each baby some one-on-one attention. Or perhaps a childcare helper can pitch in at bedtime. After earliest infancy, storytime and other bedtime routines and rituals (also see Chapter 6) for both children can be

Twins and multiples go through phases of night waking, just as singletons do. However, although there are few scientific studies on separation anxiety in children of multiple births, parents of twins and multiples claim informally that their children—like later-borns—seem to be less troubled by separation anxiety than singletons, especially firstborn single children.

combined to take place in neutral territory, such as the living room, then the youngsters can be separated at the moment of actually going to bed.

On the other side of the fence, many parents prefer to keep twins and multiples together because, as they get to know each other, one will comfort the other at those difficult times when parents have something urgent to attend to and cannot spare an arm for one child, let alone two. In addition, parents often find that if twins (or more) share a room from the start, they learn to tune each other out and one is less likely to wake up the other with crying.

In any case, once the babies get used to one another's company, which may happen as early as 4 months and certainly will between 6 and 9 months, they may cry for each other and refuse to be parted at night. Even if they have slept separately until now, they may want to share a room for at least a year or two. Far better to follow their lead and have them sleep contentedly with two cribs or beds in one room than to insist on separate rooms before they are ready.

Musical Chairs

More often than not, parents of multiples have fewer bedrooms than children. If the youngsters are spread out over two or three bedrooms, it may be an idea to switch beds every few months so the children can enjoy a change of nighttime company and you can also determine the best combinations to ensure peaceful nights for everyone. Two particular children together, for example, may excite each other, but may stay calmer if they are split up to share bedrooms with other siblings, whether identical in age or older members of the family.

CHAPTER 10

Solving
Common Problems

Psychologists use the term "sleep associations" when they talk about the behaviors and sensory factors that help us grow drowsy and fall asleep. For example, you may have taught your child to fall asleep on her own by calming her with stories and music, placing her still awake in her crib with a small, soft toy for company, whispering "good night," and leaving a night-light on. Your baby thus developed helpful sleep associations: a regular routine, feeling safe and sleepy in her crib, a transitional object, and a dim light to orient her. Now that she's 8 months old, she can comfort herself and go back to sleep after her numerous nighttime arousals. Of course, if she wakes up and really cries, you go into her room to see if she needs attention.

> *Waking at night is rarely a problem. We all do it, from newborns to the very oldest among us. The hard part is getting back to sleep.*

Your best friend, by contrast, always nursed and rocked her baby at bedtime until he fell asleep at the breast. Whenever she heard a whimper, she ran into his room, turned on the light, and picked him up to see what was the matter. Then she nursed and rocked again to help him get back to sleep. She tried giving him a pacifier, but it fell out of his mouth when he got sleepy. Because he couldn't find it on his own, he cried, becoming wide awake and upset. Nursing was the only way to calm him down. Besides, he still needed the rocking. This baby developed sleep associations that didn't work for his family: He was never left to fall asleep on his own; he couldn't comfort himself unless his mother nursed and rocked him; when he was only stirring in his sleep, bright lights were turned on and he was lifted out of his bed, which made him wide awake. The vicious circle continued with more nursing and rocking. Now he's 8 months old and still not sleeping through the night. After talking with their pediatrician, his parents understand that just as they taught him unhelpful sleep associations with nursing and rocking, now they have to teach him sleep associations that are more comfortable for the family, so he can learn to fall asleep on his own and the whole family can get a night's rest.

Real life is never quite so cut-and-dried as these contrasting situations. However, if the first represents an ideal to which we all aspire, the second illustrates some of the commonest pitfalls that trap parents, particularly with their first child. It's never too late to correct a mistake and establish a consistent, soothing routine. But the longer the problem is left unattended, the longer it may take to change. The wonderful thing about babies is that they are adaptable and forgiving in equal measure. Your baby can learn new ways in a week or two.

Of course, not all sleep disturbances are due to errors in parenting. Phases involving more frequent waking, night fears, and even nightmares are part of normal development. In addition, different babies have different temperaments; your first child may respond to one type of approach, your second may require the opposite tack. As long as your child develops a normally regular pattern of sleeping and napping, the family is likely to weather occasional disturbances without losing too much sleep over them.

No Time to Sleep

Infants are often wakeful at night around the time they reach major milestones. They may also seem impatient and irritable during the daytime. It's as if the youngster is so eager to master a new skill—be it standing up or walking alone—that she can't be bothered with routine activities such as eating, dressing, and sleeping.

A child who has just learned to pull himself up to a standing position by holding on to the crib bars may be particularly demanding until he also learns to get down again. Unless he doesn't mind tumbling to the mattress, he may call his parents over and over to help him down, only to repeat the performance minutes later. You can teach your new *Homo erectus* to get down

PARENTS MAY PROJECT THEIR OWN FEELINGS ONTO CRYING BABIES

Psychologists who have studied the behavior of thousands of children caution parents not to over-interpret babies' crying. An older child can explain her feelings. But parents don't always know why a young baby cries. What they hear, therefore, may reflect their own moods and concerns rather than their baby's wants. A baby who howls just after being put into her crib may be only letting off steam. She's not necessarily saying, "I'm lonely," or "You're cruel to abandon me," or even, "You'll have to listen to this crying forever." Resist the urge to rush back and rescue her. Your baby may just feel like vocalizing before she settles down to sleep. Or, as often in the latter half of the first year, your baby may be expressing disquiet due to the beginnings of separation anxiety.

by gently supporting him while pressing firmly against the backs of his knees until they buckle. Practice this maneuver during the day. Your baby will soon get the hang of it. When he does, he will again be able to relax and settle for sleep or go on to a new phase: perhaps babbling his newest sounds or getting ready to walk alone.

INFANTS NEED TO LEARN TO SETTLE THEMSELVES

Although hearing an infant cry evokes a feeling of urgency in all of us, we need to help our babies learn gradually to settle themselves. Once you have made sure that your baby is all right, if it is naptime or bedtime you can leave her alone for a while even though she continues to cry. However, don't let her cry for more than 10 minutes without checking on her. If this pattern of crying persists, reconsider your bedtime routines and schedules. A talk with your pediatrician could be helpful.

MANAGING A MIDNIGHT RAMBLER

The first time your toddler climbs out of his crib, he takes a major leap forward in his ability to be independent. Suddenly, he can come and go as he pleases; he's no longer totally dependent on grown-ups. For a normally active youngster, this breakthrough can happen anytime from around age 1 year onward. The first signal that it has arrived may be the sound of a jarring bump in your child's room, followed by mingled wails of surprise, pain, and fright. Or you may simply awaken to the presence of a ghostly little figure beside your bed.

Several questions arise with this new stage of mobility. First, will your child continue to sleep in a crib? Or is it time to switch to a bed? And whether he remains with his crib awhile longer or graduates to a bed, how do you persuade him to stay there the whole night through?

You may be able to keep a toddler in a crib for a few months longer by lowering the crib mattress as far as it will go, so that the rail is too high to climb over. (The top of the rail should be at least 26 inches from the mattress.) It's also essential to remove crib bumpers and bulky stuffed toys, which youngsters use to get a leg up; in fact, bumpers should be removed as soon as your child can get up on all fours—starting at around 4 months—and large stuffed toys should never be placed in the crib (for tips on crib safety, see p. 49). Some parents resort to crib tents, available commercially, which form a ceiling over the top of the crib. These products may be dangerous because, in an emergency, the attachments can be time-consuming to take off. In addition, many children feel uncomfortably confined when their movements are restricted in this way.

BUNK BEDS

Children love bunk beds, but they can be dangerous. The child in the top bunk can fall out, and the child in the lower bunk can be injured if the upper bunk collapses. If you accept these risks and decide to install bunk beds anyway, take the following precautions to keep your child safe.

1. Do not allow a child under age 6 to sleep in the top bunk. A child younger than 6 does not have the coordination to climb safely or to keep from falling out.

2. Place the bunk beds in a corner, with walls on two sides. This not only helps to brace the beds, but also eliminates two out of the four possible sites for falling out.

3. Make sure the top mattress fits snugly within the frame and cannot ride over the edge.

4. Attach a ladder to the top bunk. Place a night-light so your child can see the ladder.

5. Install a guardrail on the top bunk, with a space no wider than 3$\frac{1}{2}$ inches between the guardrail and the side of the bunk. Check to make sure your child can't roll under the guardrail when the mattress is pressed down by the weight of his body. Replace the mattress or place a thick pad under the old mattress if necessary.

6. Check that the mattress is supported by wires or slats that run directly underneath and are fastened in place at both ends. A mattress held up only by the bed frame or unsecured slats could fall through to the lower bunk.

7. If you separate the bunks into twin beds, remove all dowels and connectors.

8. To stop children from falling and avoid weakening the structure, do not allow children to jump or roughhouse on either bunk.

MAKING CLIMBERS SAFER. If your child is going to climb out of bed, whether you want him to or not, let him know the only time that climbing out is acceptable: namely, when sleep or nap time is over. In addition, you should make his room as safe and hazard-free as you can. While you are waiting to buy a new bed, make a bed on the floor with the crib mattress. Clear away furniture and large toys, like rocking horses, that could injure your child if he fell against them. You may also need to install a safety gate across your toddler's bedroom door to keep him from wandering when you are not awake. Install childproof latches on chests of drawers or tape drawers shut so they can't be pulled out and used as steps.

MANAGING THE SWITCH TO A BED. On transferring permanently to a bed, your toddler may have a heady sense of freedom the first few nights. Luckily, most youngsters are happy to "graduate," and stay in their beds more willingly than they did in their cribs. However, for a few, to prevent them from turning into confirmed night owls, the transition has to be managed closely (also see p. 94). The best way is to continue with the same bedtime routine you have used since your child first joined the family (see Chapter 6, "Bedtime Routines and Rituals"), and repeat the following steps:

1. When you end your routine, tell your child to stay in bed until you come for her.
2. If she gets out of bed, calmly and quietly lead her back and tell her she must stay in bed.
3. When she gets back into bed, reward her by telling her briefly what a good girl she is for being there, then leave the room.

But don't kid yourself that the struggle is over. Be prepared to repeat steps 1 and 2 as many times as you have to for several nights in a row. Twenty "farewell appearances" in one evening is by no means an unusual number. Above all, stay calm and keep interactions with your child on a low-key level. The aim is to reward her with praise for staying in bed, and not for getting out. Youngsters tend to feel, as many commercial advertisers do, that any attention is better than none. If getting out of bed brings your toddler extra attention—even negative attention, by making

If at First You Don't Succeed...

? *We have a 3-year-old son and not one night goes by without his waking up and coming into our room to sleep. I'll bring him back to his room three or four times before I finally give up and lose the battle. Is there any way we can all get a good night's sleep?*

Your question suggests that you already know the answer. As you say, you "finally give up and lose the battle," and in doing so you teach your 3-year-old that persistence is the key to success. He knows that after three or four trial runs, he will eventually get what he wants. To reprogram the behavior, you will have to demonstrate similar persistence, and return your son to his bed every time he gets out. This may mean a higher level of sleep disturbance for several nights, but your youngster will catch on. If you prefer to head him off before he reaches your bedroom, try hanging a small bell on his door to wake you when he leaves his room. And if he is unusually persistent, you may have to stay awake long enough to train him with the "in bed—door open, out of bed—door closed" approach (see p. 176). If you use this method, don't forget to shut his bedroom door after he's asleep, as a fire safety measure.

you angry—she'll do it again and again. By contrast, if you keep the atmosphere quiet and even boring, the excitement of getting out will soon pall.

While respecting your toddler's newfound mobility, insist on the rule that once it's time for sleep, people have to stay in bed until morning. Avoid rewarding bedroom breakouts, such as by allowing your child to climb into your bed or join the members of the family who are still up. Instead, praise her in the morning for having stayed in bed all night.

A Four-Year-Old Night Owl

? *Our daughter, age 4¹/₂, is a night owl. We manage to get her into bed by 9:00 and turn the lights out by 10:00, but she often plays in bed until after midnight. Needless to say, it's difficult to rouse her for childcare at 8:00 the next morning, although she is fairly alert by the time she arrives at school. She naps on weekday afternoons but not on the weekends; however, even then she will not go to sleep earlier. Do night owl tendencies run in families?*

While the world seems to be generally divided between early-rising larks and late-retiring owls, there is debate about the influence of nature versus nurture on the development of these characteristics. In any case, a natural tendency can be modified by scheduling that regulates the body's circadian rhythms (see p. 6). These rhythms, which play a key role in our readiness for sleep, naturally function according to the 24-hour solar cycle of daylight and darkness. But if not regulated by events that take place about the same time every day—exposure to light and darkness, eating, sleeping, and waking

SHUTTING THE DOOR. It's never acceptable to keep a child's bedroom door locked at night. In case of an emergency, such as a fire, the child cannot get out of a locked bedroom and the parents may be unable to unlock the door in time. Moreover, a child who is forcibly kept in her room behind a locked door will not develop the self-control to stay there willingly. And if a resentful child is forced to stay unsupervised in her room, she may injure herself or damage objects in the room.

However, when you are dealing with a persistent nighttime rambler, the door can be a useful aid. Many youngsters prefer to go to sleep with the bedroom door ajar. Tell your child that as long as she remains in bed, the door can stay partly open. The in the morning—the circadian rhythms tend to shift steadily later.

Your daughter's late sleep phase (the hours spent asleep and awake) and daily rhythms probably caused no problems when she was younger, but now her schedules for rest and activity are in conflict. Her cycles should be adjusted (see p. 120) to help her fall asleep earlier and, consequently, wake up better rested to get more out of her school day.

The most important stimulus for the sleep/wake cycle is waking in the morning. Therefore, in resetting your child's schedule, keep strictly to the same wake-up time every day, weekends included, and make bedtime 15 minutes earlier every 2 or 3 days until you have settled at the target bedtime (see chart on p. 121). While this adjustment is going on, limit afternoon naps to an hour. Avoid very stimulating play near bedtime. By age 4, many children are ready to give up naps. Once your daughter's sleep phase is reset, you may find that she goes without her afternoon nap in favor of an earlier time to fall asleep. It is often necessary to keep the same schedule 7 days a week to prevent relapses.

moment she gets out of bed, the door will be shut. As with any approach to discipline, this one won't work unless you consistently follow up your words with actions. At the end of the bedtime routine, allow one last chance to go to the toilet or have a drink of water. After you leave the bedroom, stay near the door so that you can respond immediately. If your youngster gets out of bed, shut the door at once; when she gets back into bed, open it. The lesson will take only if you respond every time your child makes a move. As long as you do so, your child will probably need no more than two or three nights to learn to stay in bed. When your child is asleep and before you go to bed, shut the doors to all sleeping rooms. The American Academy of Pediatrics recommends that doors to sleeping rooms be kept shut, but not locked, at night as a fire safety measure.

TEETHING

For as long as babies have awakened their parents at night, teething has taken the blame. Yet when researchers tried to find links between symptoms and teething, they couldn't identify any. What actually happens is that babies' first teeth generally appear between 5 and 10 months. This coincides with the onset of waking and fearfulness due to separation anxiety, a normal stage in your child's development (see p. 19). It's easy to leap to a conclusion and see a cause-effect relationship where none exists.

A baby who is teething may be mildly irritable and drool a lot. The gums around the emerging teeth may be swollen and tender, and your baby may not want to nurse. However, she may want to bite on something firm, such as a teething toy, her fist, or your finger. Give her objects to chew on—teething rings or hard, unsweetened teething crackers. Frozen teething toys should not be used; extreme cold can injure your baby's mouth and cause more

CLEARING YOUR CHILD'S STUFFED-UP NOSE

- A cool-mist humidifier in your child's room may help to keep his nasal passages clear.

- Use a bulb syringe to suction out the mucus anytime your baby's nose is blocked and especially before feedings. Your pediatrician may recommend saltwater nose drops to thin the mucus and make it easier to suction.

- Don't treat your child's stuffy nose with medicated nose drops or sprays. Although sold over the counter for the relief of congestion, these products can actually increase congestion after only a few days' use, with a rebound effect that is more uncomfortable and more difficult to treat than the original problem. Use medications only as your pediatrician advises.

discomfort. The pain relievers intended to be rubbed on a baby's gums aren't helpful; a teething baby drools so much that the medication is quickly washed away. In addition, pediatricians warn that such medications can numb the back of the throat and interfere with the baby's ability to swallow. If your baby is clearly uncomfortable, talk to your pediatrician about a possible course of action.

When your baby's teeth are coming through, she may also have a very slight increase in temperature. But if the rectal temperature goes above the upper limit of normal—100.4°F (38°C)—it's not due to teething. If your baby has symptoms such as fever, vomiting, or diarrhea while teething, consult your pediatrician to find out whether she has a medical condition requiring treatment.

If your teething baby is irritable, try to make her comfortable, but keep to your usual bedtime routine. Changing the routine, even for a few nights, may only lead to sleep troubles.

ILLNESS AND RECUPERATION

Babies and young children may have problems sleeping when they are sick. Their rest is broken by discomfort due to fever, pain, coughing, runny or stuffy nose, and other symptoms. A stuffed-up nose can be particularly irksome, because when a baby is forced to breathe through the mouth, he has trouble feeding and he can't soothe himself by sucking his thumb. A sick child usually has trouble falling asleep and staying asleep. This is a pity, because a long, restful sleep often seems to help a youngster turn the corner from feeling ill to getting better.

For as long as symptoms are present, your sick child will need soothing, cuddling, possibly frequent clean-ups, drinks, medication, and whatever comfort you can provide to help her sleep. Of course, call your pediatrician if your baby under 3 months has a fever, with rectal temperature above 100.4°F (38°C), or if your child has severe or persistent symptoms at any age.

As soon as your child is well again, pick up your normal nighttime routine. Lights go out at the regular time and everybody stays quietly in bed unless there's a real problem needing attention. If you're attentive when your child needs you, and con-

DAY FOR NIGHT

? *Our preschooler doesn't seem to be able to tell the difference between day and night. She naps for long periods during the day, and then wants to play and have snacks when we need to sleep. How do we turn her around?*

This problem can develop quite quickly in an infant who sleeps later and consequently gets tired later for several days in a row. However, in an older child, it is usually the result of irregular schedules for sleeping, waking, napping, and mealtimes over an extended period. In time, the youngster's circadian rhythms, or body clock (see Chapter 1), shift in such a way that her normal cycles of body temperature, hunger, and activity level are all off-kilter. Consequently, she cannot fall asleep at the normal times.

Because our circadian rhythms tend to shift progressively later over the 24-hour day, they have to be maintained by events that occur at the same time each day: waking in the morning, eating,

sistent but not inflexible about limits, she will go along with the system. A young baby may continue to wake up periodically during the night because she has quickly become used to the extra attention and cuddling she enjoyed while sick. However, your calm and consistent approach will help her get back to the usual routine. Once she has had a few bouts with the common childhood illnesses—colds, ear infection, or gastroenteritis—she will understand that rules can be bent when a person doesn't feel well. She'll be glad to get back to the normal routine as she feels better.

BED-WETTING

Most children are fully toilet trained between ages 3 and 4, managing to stay dry at night about 6 months to a year after napping, exposure to light and dark, and settling down for sleep at night. If there isn't a consistent routine, our bodies don't know when to sleep and when to wake up.

To reset your child's internal clock, set up a regular daily schedule with times for getting up, meals and snacks, naps, and going to bed. Explain the new system to your child and post a wall chart that you and she can check off, at least for the first 2 weeks or so, until you have established a rhythm. When your child wakes up at night, go to her room to provide reassurance but keep the lights dim and speak only as much as you have to. Don't provide snacks or let her get up and play. If necessary, use the "odd jobs" or "in bed—door open, out of bed—door closed" technique (see pp. 130, 176) to emphasize that your child must stay in bed. During the period of adjustment, limit naps to no more than 1 to 2 hours a day. Once she's back on a regular schedule of sleeping at night, she may give up daytime naps or simply enjoy a quiet time, without sleeping, during the afternoon. Keep the schedule the same 7 days a week.

achieving daytime control over urination. However, as many as 15 percent of youngsters continue to wet the bed up to age 5 or even later. Boys are more likely to wet the bed to an older age than girls. In most cases, the child is simply a bit later than average in developing the ability to wake up when he senses his bladder is full. The problem generally clears up as the child matures.

Persistent bed-wetting tends to run in families; 15 to 20 percent of children who wet the bed have a family history of bed-wetting. In fact, if both parents wet the bed as youngsters, there's a greater than 50 percent chance that their child will wet the bed to an older age. Researchers suspect, therefore, that bed-wetting is linked to a genetic trait.

Not all children who wet the bed have problems of night waking. Indeed, many of them sleep soundly through several wetting episodes a night. They may call for attention only when they become chilled by clammy bedclothes and sleepwear.

If your child continues to wet the bed after age 6, ask your pediatrician to evaluate the situation and recommend treatment, if necessary. When a child wets the bed again after being dry for 6 months or longer, the youngster may need treatment. The cause could be either a physical problem—such as a urinary tract infection or diabetes mellitus—or emotional stress.

CALL YOUR PEDIATRICIAN IF YOUR CHILD HAS ANY OF THE FOLLOWING SIGNS OF PHYSICAL ILLNESS:

- Redness or rash in the genital area.

- Pain or burning on urination.

- Cloudy or pinkish urine; bloodstains on underpants or sleepwear.

- Straining during urination, a narrow stream of urine, or dribbling after urination.

- Fever (temperature 100.4°F [38°C] or higher, along with other symptoms such as headache or vomiting).

- Daytime as well as nighttime wetting.

- **Call your pediatrician at once if your child has any of the following signs of dehydration: dry mouth; sunken eyes; few tears when crying; lethargy; wrinkled skin.**

A child may wet the bed again when faced with a stressful situation. Typical stress triggers include starting school for the first time, feeling pushed aside by the arrival of a baby in the family, or becoming aware of discord between the parents. If your normally dry child wets the bed during a time of stress, reassure him, provide the emotional support he needs, and try to reduce the stress. Without making a fuss about it, protect the mattress

BED-WETTING IN A NINE-YEAR-OLD

? *My 9-year-old son wets his bed. His father also wet until fifth grade. I know that my son needs to sleep, but I worry about him lying in a wet bed all night. I used to get him up to go to the bathroom but it made for very unrestful nights. How do I best handle this situation?*

If your school-age son is not upset at having a wet bed, don't make it an issue; he won't suffer any ill effects from lying on a warm, damp sheet. As you point out, getting your youngster up to use the bathroom only disturbed everybody's sleep and probably didn't help stop him from wetting the bed.

Remind your son to urinate one final time before lights out each night. And although restricting fluids in the evening is no longer thought to prevent bed-wetting, it's probably not helpful if your child has a big drink just before bedtime. Certainly, he should not have caffeine-containing drinks, such as iced teas, colas, and other soft drinks, which increase urine production.

Protect the mattress with a dampproof sheet and disposable absorbent pads. Encourage your son to help change the bedclothes each morning just before or after his shower. Reassure him that he's not to blame for the bed-wetting; it is probably a family trait that he will outgrow. If he's anxious about staying dry at night, seek your pediatrician's advice.

with a moistureproof sheet. When accidents occur, let your child help with changing the bedclothes, but don't turn it into a punishment. If he feels more secure wearing absorbent pull-ups to bed, let him do so; however, once a child has said good-bye to nighttime diapers, he's not likely to want to take this backward step. Let other family members know that teasing will not be tolerated. If the bed-wetting persists longer than 2 weeks, or you cannot identify the source of stress, arrange an appointment with your pediatrician to see if further attention is required.

TREATMENT FOR BED-WETTING. For a child older than 6 who wets the bed fairly often and who is not suffering from a medical condition or emotional difficulties, the following plan may be helpful. Before starting, discuss it with your pediatrician to make sure it's the right approach for your youngster.

- Talk over the problem with your child, letting him know that you understand and that it's not his fault.
- Don't forbid fluids at night but discourage your youngster from drinking large amounts at bedtime—and no caffeine-containing drinks such as soda pop or iced tea.
- Remind him to go to the bathroom one last time before the lights are turned out.
- Set up a chart with stars or stickers to reward him for dry nights, but avoid any suggestion of punishment for wet nights. Promise a modest treat once he has accumulated a certain number of stickers, and promptly follow through with the treat.

BE WARY OF MAIL-ORDER TREATMENTS

Don't be lured by claims for the bed-wetting cures advertised in mail-order catalogs and other publications. Your pediatrician can supply reliable advice about treatments for bed-wetting.

Between 80 and 85 percent of youngsters are helped by this method of positive reinforcement. If there's no improvement after 3 months, talk to your pediatrician again to plan the next phase of treatment. A bed-wetting alarm is the most effective and long-lasting treatment. Medication to alter your child's sleep/wake cycle may be prescribed. Or your pediatrician may prescribe a nasal spray containing a hormone that normally helps to conserve fluid when the body is dehydrated. Given to prevent bed-wetting,

MASTURBATION IN A YOUNG CHILD

? We adopted our 5-year-old son at age 3¹/2. He frequently masturbates while in bed. One book we consulted described this as "infantile pseudomasturbation." Is it simply a comforting habit—like thumb-sucking—that will recede as he develops, or could it indicate a more serious psychological problem?

Masturbation, or stimulation of the genitals, is normal and common among both boys and girls. For most young children, masturbation is just a comforting sensation. Parents should neither discourage nor call unnecessary attention to the activity. However, if your son stimulates himself in public, teach him the social rules by having him go to a private area for a little while and rejoin the family when he feels ready.

At times, excessive masturbation or a public display may be a sign that a child is under emotional strain, has poor impulse control, is unduly preoccupied with sex, or is not receiving the emotional comfort he or she needs. In some cases it may indicate that a child has been sexually abused. Make sure that your child does not have access to sexual material, and is not exposed to inappropriate nudity in your home.

If there is a compulsive quality to your child's activity, if he has signs of emotional disturbance—such as fecal soiling, aggressiveness, or social withdrawal— or if you have any concerns about the influence of other children or adults with whom your child has been spending time, consult your pediatrician, who will examine your child and recommend an appropriate course of action.

the hormone can trick the body into acting as if it has no fluid to spare, thus suppressing the urge to urinate.

A very small number of children don't seem to benefit from treatment for bed-wetting. However, almost all of them are free of the problem by adolescence. No more than one adult out of 100 has persistent bed-wetting. Until your child outgrows bed-wetting, he will need plenty of emotional support from his family. Counseling from your pediatrician or another health professional may also be helpful. Even if treatments are unsuccessful, your youngster should be encouraged to keep trying to stay dry at night by avoiding large drinks in the evening and using the bathroom one last time before settling down to sleep. As a general rule, he should avoid drinks containing caffeine, which can stimulate urination. Coffee and tea are obvious sources of caffeine; however, even decaffeinated coffees and teas contain some caffeine. Colas and many other soft drinks also contain caffeine. Check nutritional information labels carefully. Exercises to increase your youngster's bladder capacity may also be helpful; ask your pediatrician's advice.

CHAPTER 11

Changes at Adolescence

Youngsters' need for sleep does not decrease as they mature into adolescents; however, the amount of sleep they actually get tends to fall. The reason? In no particular order: normal hormonal changes, homework, sports, jobs, dating, computers, malls, TV, and just hanging out. There aren't enough hours in the day for all this and sleeping, too.

A major change in the nightly sleep cycle with adolescence is a decrease in the length of time spent in stages III and IV sleep (see pp. 8–10). When compared with sleep patterns in children before puberty, these deep stages of non-REM sleep are shorter by a little more than one-third overall.

Teenagers need between 9 and 10 hours of sleep a night. What they get on average is nearer to 7 hours. Typically, adolescents sleep less than they need to on weeknights, then try to pay back the accumulated sleep debt by sleeping longer on weekends. The most common sleep disorder in teenagers, therefore, is a sleep phase shift (also see p. 190) brought about by an irregular schedule with progressively later sleep and wake times. Other problems may also appear for the first time during the teen years.

> *Among the hallmarks of physical maturation at puberty are a decrease in sleep latency—that is, a shorter interval between the time a teenager gets into bed and when she falls asleep—and an increase in daytime sleepiness.*

Hormones and Sleep

Throughout childhood, growth hormone is secreted in regular pulses around the clock, with the highest blood levels occurring during sleep. However, a unique characteristic of adolescence is a spurt in the output of growth hormone and gonadotropins—the hormones that regulate the development and function of the sexual organs—at the end of each sleep period. This surge does not occur at any other stage of life.

Adolescents who have experienced major weight loss as a result of the eating disorder anorexia nervosa do not have the normal surge in gonadotropin secretion with sleep. The pattern may also be disturbed in other conditions involving substantial weight loss, such as chronic illness. As a result of this interruption in growth hormone release, a youngster who develops anorexia early in puberty may gain height poorly or not at all until the condition is dealt with. If anorexia sets in later, when growth is practically complete, height may not be markedly affected.

Sleep Problems at Adolescence

NARCOLEPSY. Narcolepsy is one of several sleep problems that may emerge at adolescence. A teenager with narcolepsy becomes irresistibly sleepy during the daytime and has bouts of REM sleep during normal waking hours. In the vast majority of cases, simple drowsiness and fatigue do not represent narcolepsy. Usually, they mean that a youngster is not getting enough sleep at night or is experiencing side effects from medications. To make a firm diagnosis of narcolepsy, a doctor looks for several symptoms in addition to drowsiness and may order a sleep study. A person with narcolepsy may have recurrent, frightening visual images, called hypnagogic hallucinations, just before sleep. Youngsters with narcolepsy may suddenly lose control of their muscles and fall to the ground while remaining fully awake. This condition is called cataplexy. Finally, those with narcolepsy may experience sleep paralysis, the feeling of being unable to move or breathe despite being conscious, while falling asleep or on waking.

Although narcolepsy is sometimes seen in the early school years, it is more likely to occur in adolescence and early adulthood. Narcolepsy is a lifelong condition and requires lifelong treatment to relieve the symptoms. In some cases, the sleepiness becomes less intense over time and some of the symptoms disappear altogether, even without treatment.

TEENAGE SLEEP BINGES

Adolescents may make up for inadequate sleep and erratic weekday sleep schedules by bingeing on sleep during weekends. It's not unusual for a teenager to sleep until noon and follow up with periodic naps over the course of a weekend. However, if your teenager is regularly sleeping unusually late or taking long naps on weekdays as well, talk to her or arrange an appointment with your pediatrician. Excessive sleep may be a sign that a youngster is suffering from a mood disorder or is abusing substances.

APNEA. An adolescent who complains of sleeping poorly and is unusually tired during the daytime may have sleep apnea. This condition occurs when the youngster stops breathing repeatedly during the night, partly wakes, and usually resumes breathing with a loud snort or choking sound. Other features associated with the condition include breathing through the mouth and morning headache. Enlargement of the tonsils and adenoid tissue is often the explanation. Other causes include an unusually small chin, large tongue, and other problems with the nerves and muscles of the face and head. Being overweight increases the risk (also see p. 65), but even a wiry adolescent may develop apnea as a result of relaxation of the throat muscles during REM sleep.

If you notice unusual snoring or noisy breathing and your teenager is fatigued and irritable, arrange for a checkup with your pediatrician.

SLEEP-PHASE SHIFT. A shift in the sleep phase—that is, the hours spent in sleep out of each 24-hour period—frequently occurs

SLEEP DIFFICULTIES MAY INDICATE MENTAL HEALTH PROBLEMS

? *Our 16-year-old daughter has always had difficulty falling asleep although, once asleep, she has no trouble staying asleep. We recently found out that for the past 3 years, she has been experimenting with alcohol and drugs, and a psychiatric disorder has also been diagnosed. She is now in treatment for these problems. Can sleep difficulties be symptoms of mental or emotional problems?*

A marked change in sleeping habits may be a signal that attention is required. It's important to seek your pediatrician's advice if your adolescent:

- Is sleeping much longer or much less than usual.

- Often wakes in the middle of the night and cannot get back to sleep.

- Has phases of low moods and oversleeping alternating with periods when she is erratic, hyperactive, argumentative, and sleeping little.

In most cases, problems of wakefulness occur because the youngster is simply in the habit of both going to sleep and waking up late. Adolescents, particularly, fall into this routine. A teenager may also lie awake worrying about how to resolve a temporary situation or fear. In this case, gentle questioning may lead her to say what's on her mind.

with adolescence, partly because of hormonal influences on sleep and partly because the teenager stays up and gets up later, whether to take part in social activities, to work, or to distance himself from his family. If the shift interferes with routine activities, including school and family obligations, it may be necessary to restore the earlier sleep phase by gradually stepping back the

Irregular sleep habits combined with inexperience behind the wheel too often are lethal for teenage drivers and others on the roads. The American Medical Association Council for Scientific Affairs is alarmed about the role of sleep disorders and fatigue in motor vehicle crashes. The council encourages measures to increase drivers' awareness of the dangers of driving when fatigued and has called for studies into ways of preventing such tragedies.

Sleep experts recommend that driver education courses include specific warnings about drowsy driving. One prominent researcher put it this way:

> Drowsiness, that feeling when the eyelids are trying to close and we cannot seem to keep them open, is the last step before we fall asleep, not the first. If at this moment we let sleep come, it will arrive instantly. When driving a car, or in any hazardous situation, the first wave of drowsiness should be a dramatic warning. Get out of harm's way instantly! Drowsiness is red alert!

time of going to bed while keeping the wake-up time constant, even on weekends (for a suggested schedule, see *Night Owls*, pp. 120-121).

INSOMNIA. Insomnia that makes it difficult to fall asleep is also associated with the sleep-phase shift. It can often be improved if a youngster adjusts his schedule and keeps to regular times for waking up and going to bed. When insomnia involves early morning waking, the teenager may be suffering from depression and/or anxiety. As the underlying condition is dealt with, the insomnia generally improves.

Adolescents frequently have trouble getting to sleep because of the amount of caffeine they consume daily in the form of soft drinks and chocolate. Colas are obvious culprits, but other soft drinks also contain substantial amounts of caffeine. This stimu-

If your adolescent daughter is suddenly sleeping much more or less than usual, and is faint, nauseated, or vomiting for several days in a row, she may be pregnant or fearful that she is pregnant. If you have reason to believe she is sexually active and could be pregnant, discuss it with her calmly and consult your pediatrician without delay.

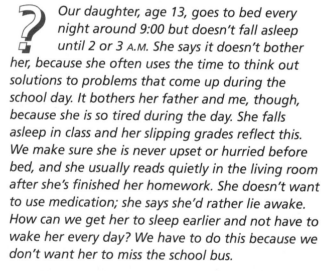

A Teenager Has to Take Control

Our daughter, age 13, goes to bed every night around 9:00 but doesn't fall asleep until 2 or 3 A.M. She says it doesn't bother her, because she often uses the time to think out solutions to problems that come up during the school day. It bothers her father and me, though, because she is so tired during the day. She falls asleep in class and her slipping grades reflect this. We make sure she is never upset or hurried before bed, and she usually reads quietly in the living room after she's finished her homework. She doesn't want to use medication; she says she'd rather lie awake. How can we get her to sleep earlier and not have to wake her every day? We have to do this because we don't want her to miss the school bus.

Your daughter has developed a late sleep phase, or sleep/wake cycle (see p. 190). It is possible to shift the sleep phase by keeping to a regular schedule for going to bed and waking up. However, the schedule for waking must be followed 7 days a week without fail; if it is ignored on weekends, the adjustment process is disrupted. The time for going to bed is lant is also an ingredient in many over-the-counter pain relievers. Teenagers with sleep problems should try cutting out soft drinks and chocolate for at least 2 weeks to see if sleeplessness gets better. In addition, they should make a habit of reading food labels, including those on soft drinks, chocolate, and candies, to avoid caffeine.

ADOLESCENT NIGHT OWLS (DELAYED SLEEP-PHASE SYNDROME). Biological changes during puberty bring about shifts in the sleep phase that encourage teenagers to stay up late (also see p. 26) and

not quite as important, so bedtimes may be a little more flexible on non-school nights.

In general, it's more difficult to shift the sleep phase in adolescents than in younger children, simply because the habit is more entrenched. A key to success is requiring that the teenager assume control over her bedtime and waking. Most of all, she must be responsible for getting up in the morning and cannot rely on you, her parents, to wake her. Put a clock-radio in your daughter's bedroom and place a backup alarm on the other side of the room or even just outside her door, so she has to make an effort to turn it off. Talk over the new plan with your daughter and explain her responsibilities, including daily setting of both alarms. Draw up a contract and have her sign it, if this method fits your family's style.

If a trial of this new system for a few weeks doesn't bring about at least a slight improvement, ask your pediatrician to evaluate the situation. Sleeping much more or much less than normal may be a symptom of an emotional condition, such as depression. Your pediatrician may raise the possibility of referral to another health professional with experience in sleep disorders.

consequently oversleep. Further complicating the matter, teenagers don't like to be told what to do, and many parents, respecting their children's urge toward independence, tend to hold back advice for fear of being accused of nagging.

If an erratic sleep schedule is causing problems with school and family activities, you may ask your teenager where she thinks the problem lies. You may also suggest that she must find it difficult to fall asleep if she is paying attention to late-night TV or radio. You can even lead her toward a solution by explaining how to shift the sleep phase back, and you can provide the tools she needs, such as a clock radio and a loud alarm. However, if the program is to work, your teenager has to want to change and be prepared to take responsibility for following a new sleep schedule, including weekend wake-ups, on her own.

Occasionally, an adolescent may adopt a late sleep phase to cover up a deeper problem such as school avoidance. If your teenager is having problems with schoolwork or social issues along with a change in her sleep schedule, arrange an appointment with your pediatrician. An adolescent may talk more freely with an impartial health professional than with a family member. Your pediatrician will also be able to recommend an appropriate course of action.

Sleep Centers

Following is a partial list of sleep treatment centers that are accredited by the American Sleep Disorders Association.

Alabama
- Sleep-Wake Disorders Center
University of Alabama at
　Birmingham
1713 6th Avenue South
CPM Building, Room 270
Birmingham AL 35233-0018
Tel. 205-934-7110

Alaska
- Sleep Disorders Center
Providence Alaska Medical
　Center
3200 Providence Drive
P.O. Box 196604
Anchorage AK 99519-6604
Tel. 907-261-3650

Arizona
- Sleep Disorders Center
University of Arizona
1501 North Campbell Avenue
Tucson AZ 85724
Tel. 520-694-6112

Arkansas
- Pediatric Sleep Disorders
Arkansas Children's Hospital
800 Marshall Street
Little Rock AR 72202-3591
Tel. 501-320-1893

California
- UCLA Sleep Disorders
　Center
24-221 Center for Health
　Sciences
Box 957069
Los Angeles CA 90095-7069
Tel. 310-206-8005
- Sleep Disorders Clinic
UCSF Stanford University
　Medical Center
401 Quarry Road
Stanford CA 94305
Tel. 650-723-6601

Colorado
- National Jewish/University
　of Colorado Sleep Center
1400 Jackson Street, A105
Denver CO 80206
Tel. 303-398-1523

Connecticut
- Gaylord-Yale Sleep Services
New Haven Branch
1 Long Wharf Drive
New Haven CT 06511
Tel. 203-624-3140

Delaware

■ Sleep Disorders Center
Christiana Care Health System
Wilmington Hospital
501 West 14th Street
Wilmington DE 19899
Tel. 302-428-4600

District of Columbia

■ Sleep Disorders Center
5 Main Hospital
Georgetown University
    Hospital
3800 Reservoir Road NW
Washington DC 20007-2197
Tel. 202-784-3610

Florida

■ Sleep Disorders Center
Miami Children's Hospital
3200 SW 60th Court
Miami FL 33155
Tel. 305-662-8330

Georgia

■ Sleep Disorders Center
Northside Hospital
5780 Peachtree-Dunwoody
    Road
Suite 150
Atlanta GA 30342
Tel. 404-851-8135

Hawaii

■ Pulmonary Sleep Disorders
    Center
Kuakini Medical Center
347 North Kuakini Street
Honolulu HI 96817
Tel. 808-547-9156

Idaho

■ Idaho Sleep Disorders Center
St. Luke's Regional Medical
    Center
190 East Bannock Street
Boise ID 83712
Tel. 208-381-2440

Illinois

■ Sleep Disorders Center
The University of Chicago
    Hospitals
5758 South Maryland
MC9019
Chicago IL 60637
Tel. 773-702-1782

■ Sleep Disorder Service and
    Research Center
Rush-Presbyterian-St. Luke's
    Medical Center
1653 West Congress Parkway
Chicago IL 60612
Tel. 312-942-5440

Indiana

■ Sleep/Wake Disorders Center
Community Hospitals of
    Indianapolis
1500 North Ritter Avenue
Indianapolis IN 46219
Tel. 317-355-4275

Iowa

■ Sleep Disorders Center
Department of Neurology
The University of Iowa
    Hospitals and Clinics
Iowa City IA 52242
Tel. 319-356-3813

Kansas

- Sleep Disorders Center
Wesley Medical Center
550 North Hillside
Wichita KS 67214-4976
Tel. 316-688-2663

Kentucky

- Sleep Disorders Center
University of Louisville Hospital
530 South Jackson Street
Louisville KY 40202
Tel. 502-562-3792

Louisiana

- LSU Sleep Disorders Center
Louisiana State University
    Medical Center
1541 King's Highway
Shreveport LA 71130-3932
Tel. 318-675-5365

Maine

- St. Mary's Sleep Disorders
    Laboratory
St. Mary's Regional
    Medical Center
97 Campus Avenue
Lewiston ME 04240
Tel. 207-777-8959

Maryland

- The Johns Hopkins Pediatric
    Pulmonary and Sleep
    Disorders Center
600 North Wolfe Street
Baltimore MD 21287-2533
Tel. 410-955-2035

Massachusetts

- Sleep Clinic
Boston Children's Hospital
    Medical Center
300 Longwood Avenue
Boston MA 02115
Tel. 617-355-6663

Michigan

- Sleep Disorders Center
University of Michigan
    Hospitals
1500 East Medical Center
    Drive
Ann Arbor MI 48109-0117
Tel. 734-936-9068

Minnesota

- Mayo Sleep Disorders
    Center
Mayo Clinic
200 First Street Southwest
Rochester MN 55905
Tel. 507-266-8900

Mississippi

- Sleep Disorders Center
University of Mississippi
    Medical Center
2500 North State Street
Jackson MS 39216-4505
Tel. 601-984-4820

Missouri

- University of Missouri Sleep
    Disorders Center
University Hospital and Clinics
One Hospital Drive
Columbia MO 65212
Tel. 573-884-SLEEP

Montana

- The Sleep Center at
  St. Vincent Hospital
St. Vincent Hospital and
  Health Center
1233 North 30th Street
Billings MT 59101
Tel. 406-238-6815

Nebraska

- Great Plains Regional Sleep
  Physiology Center
Lincoln General Hospital
2300 South 16th Street
Lincoln NE 68502
Tel. 402-481-5338

Nevada

- Washoe Sleep Disorders
  Center and Sleep
  Laboratory
Washoe Professional Building
  and Washoe Medical Center
Sleep Management Inc.
75 Pringle Way
Suite 701
Reno NV 89502
Tel. 775-328-4700

New Hampshire

- Sleep Disorders Center
Dartmouth-Hitchcock Medical
  Center
One Medical Center Drive
Lebanon NH 03756
Tel. 603-650-7534

New Jersey

- Comprehensive Sleep
  Disorders Center
Robert Wood Johnson
  University Hospital
UMDNJ-Robert Wood
  Johnson Medical School
One Robert Wood Johnson
  Place
New Brunswick NJ 08903-
  2601
Tel. 732-937-8683

New Mexico

- University Hospital Sleep
  Disorders Center
4775 Indian School Road NE
Suite 307
Albuquerque NM 87110
Tel. 505-272-6101

New York

- The Sleep Disorders Center
Columbia-Presbyterian
  Medical Center
161 Fort Washington Avenue
New York NY 10032
Tel. 212-305-1860

- Sleep Disorders Center
State University of New York
  at Stony Brook
University Hospital
MR 120 A
Stony Brook NY 11794-7139
Tel. 516-444-2916

■ Capital Region Sleep/Wake
  Disorders Center
Pine West Plaza No. 1
Washington Avenue Extension
Albany NY 12205
Tel. 518-464-9999

North Carolina

■ Carolinas Sleep Services
University Hospital
P.O. Box 560727
8800 North Tryon Street
Charlotte NC 28256
Tel. 704-548-5855

Ohio

■ The Cleveland Clinic
  Foundation
Sleep Disorders Center
9500 Euclid Avenue
Desk S-51
Cleveland OH 44195
Tel. 216-444-2165

■ Sleep Disorders Center
The Ohio State University
  Medical Center
Rhodes Hall, S1039
410 West 10th Avenue
Columbus OH 43210-1228
Tel. 614-293-8296

Oklahoma

■ Sleep Disorders Center of
  Oklahoma
Integris Health
4401 South Western Avenue
Oklahoma City OK 73109
Tel. 405-636-7700

Oregon

■ Legacy Good Samaritan
  Sleep Disorders Center
Neurology, N-450
1015 Northwest 22nd Avenue
Portland OR 97210
Tel. 503-413-7540

Pennsylvania

■ Penn Center for Sleep
  Disorders
University of Pennsylvania
  Medical Center
3400 Spruce Street
11 Gates West
Philadelphia PA 19104
Tel. 215-662-7772

■ Pulmonary Sleep Evaluation
  Laboratory
University of Pittsburgh
  Medical Center
Montefiore University Hospital
3459 Fifth Avenue, S639
Pittsburgh PA 15213
Tel. 412-692-2880

South Carolina

■ Sleep Disorders Center
Greenville Memorial Hospital
701 Grove Road
Greenville SC 29605
Tel. 864-455-8916

South Dakota

■ The Sleep Center
Rapid City Regional Hospital
353 Fairmont Boulevard
P.O. Box 6000
Rapid City SD 57709
Tel. 605-341-8037

Tennessee
- Sleep Disorders Center
Methodist Hospitals of
   Memphis
1265 Union Avenue
Memphis TN 38104
Tel. 901-726-REST

Texas
- Sleep Medicine Institute
Presbyterian Hospital of Dallas
8200 Walnut Hill Lane
Dallas TX 75231
Tel. 214-750-7776
- Sleep Disorders Center
Department of Psychiatry
Baylor College of Medicine
   and VA Medical Center
One Baylor Plaza
Houston TX 77030
Tel. 713-798-4886

Utah
- Primary Children's Hospital
Pulmonary Function
   Laboratory
100 North Medical Drive
Salt Lake City UT 84113
Tel. 801-588-2736

Virginia
- Sleep Disorders Center for
   Adults and Children
Sentara Norfolk General
   Hospital
600 Gresham Drive
Norfolk VA 23507
Tel. 757-668-3000

Washington
- Providence Sleep Disorders
   Center
500 17th Avenue
Department 4 West
Seattle WA 98122
Tel. 206-320-2575

West Virginia
- Sleep Disorders Center
Charleston Area Medical Center
501 Morris Street
P.O. Box 1393
Charleston WV 25325
Tel. 304-348-7507

Wisconsin
- St. Vincent Hospital Sleep
   Disorders Center
St. Vincent Hospital
P.O. Box 13508
Green Bay WI 54307-3508
Tel. 920-431-3041

Resources from the American Academy of Pediatrics

The American Academy of Pediatrics develops and produces a wide variety of public education materials that teach parents and children the importance of preventive and therapeutic medical care. These materials include books, magazines, videos, brochures and other educational resources. Examples of these materials include:

- Brochures and fact sheets on many health and parenting issues, including allergies, childcare, divorce and single parenting, growth and development, injury prevention, immunizations, learning disabilities, nutrition and fitness, sleep problems, substance abuse prevention, and media influence on young people.
- Videos on immunizations, newborn care, nutrition education, and asthma.
- First aid, child health records, and books for parents.
- The Academy's website at www.aap.org answers questions about child health and also features information on all aspects of child rearing—including injury prevention, teen dating, fears and phobias, and the use of car seats. All the information on this site has been reviewed and approved by the American Academy of Pediatrics and represents the collective opinion and experience of more than 55,000 pediatricians.

For specific information or to keep current on new AAP public education materials, visit our website or write for a free copy of the Academy's Parents Resource Guide, sending a self-addressed, stamped No. 10 envelope to:

American Academy of Pediatrics
Department PRG
P.O. Box 927
Elk Grove Village IL 60009-0927

For help in finding a qualified pediatrician or pediatric subspecialist, contact the "Pediatrician Referral Source" of the American Academy of Pediatrics by sending the name of your town (or towns nearby) and a self-addressed, stamped envelope to:

American Academy of Pediatrics
Pediatrician Referral
P.O. Box 927
Elk Grove Village IL 60009-0927